D0825003

REASONS FOR OUR RHYMES

BR
115
.H5
H47
2001

REASONS FOR OUR RHYMES

An Inquiry into the Philosophy of History

R. A. Herrera

William B. Eerdmans Publishing Company
Grand Rapids, Michigan / Cambridge, U.K.

© 2001 Wm. B. Eerdmans Publishing Co.
All rights reserved

Wm. B. Eerdmans Publishing Co.
255 Jefferson Ave. S.E., Grand Rapids, Michigan 49503 /
P.O. Box 163, Cambridge CB3 9PU U.K.

Printed in the United States of America

06 05 04 03 02 01   7 6 5 4 3 2 1

Library of Congress Cataloging-in-Publication Data

Herrera, Robert A.
Reasons for our rhymes / Robert A. Herrera.
p.   cm.
Includes bibliographical references.
ISBN 0-8028-4928-8 (pbk.: alk. paper)
1. History — Religious aspects — Christianity —
History of doctrines.   I. Title.

BR115.H5 H47 2001
901 — dc21

2001023006

www.eerdmans.com

To the memory of my beloved mother,
Olga Coll Asciego de Herrera,
and to dear Gabby

Contents

Acknowledgments

I would like to express my gratitude to my wife, Deborah, and her gifted staff at the Seton Hall School Library; to Ed Garea for his help, advice, and efforts to drag me into the twentieth century; and to the staff of the Firestone Library of Princeton University.

Introduction

History is the autobiography of a madman.

Herzen, *Doctor Krupov*

During the third millennium BC it seems that a radical newness began in human culture: history in the sense of a transmittable record of events.[1] The term 'history' itself was probably introduced by Herodotus and taken up by Thucydides and others. The ancient Greeks did not attach much importance to history, an inclination which, as Collingwood indicated, tended to harden.[2] A good example is Aristotle, who maintained that poetry was superior to history as poetry extracts a universal judgment from disparate historical events.[3] Polybius, prodded by his awareness of Rome's universal mission, moved from the recording of individual events to weaving a tapestry depicting imperial purpose.

The purpose of history as such, as Ranke stated, is to reveal the past as it truly happened.[4] However, this is no more than a point of departure for

---

1. Lewis Mumford, *Technics and Human Development* (New York: Harcourt, Brace, Jovanovich, 1967), 1:163.

2. R. G. Collingwood, *The Idea of History* (New York: Oxford Univ. Press, 1956), 29.

3. Aristotle, *Poetics* 1451b 1-7.

4. Cited by Arthur Herman, *The Idea of Decline in Western History* (New York: The Free Press, 1997), 78.

the philosophy of history. As Pieper has indicated, the philosophy of history is different from history in principle, as it asks whether the event means something over and above the merely factual.[5] It poses the question of ends, of finality, and in doing so reveals an essential relation to religion and theology that history *per se,* despising eschatology, does not possess. The boundaries between the philosophy of history and the theology of history are, at best, tenuous, and tend to merge. In any case, the term 'philosophy of history', as used to designate a particular intellectual discipline, is a latecomer, probably first employed by the Abbé Bazin in *La philosophie de l'histoire* in 1765, though it was not widely used until Voltaire[6] made it famous.

Sir Isaiah Berlin, in a well-known essay, made the distinction between two intellectual types, the hedgehog and the fox.[7] The first, the hedgehog, relates everything to a "single central vision . . . in terms of which alone all that they are and say had significance." The second, the fox, pursues many ends and is centrifugal rather than centripetal. The philosopher (theologian) of history is decidedly a hedgehog as he imposes a plot on time and interprets everything through its prism. And the plot derives its significance from its end.

However, as James Hutton stated in 1790, history has "no vestige of a beginning, no prospect of an end."[8] Because of the absence of a beginning the ancient world gave birth to several unfinished plots, pining over the long-lost Age of Saturn as did Adam remembering Eden. Ovid, in the *Metamorphosis,* indicates that in the Age of Saturn good faith and virtue were cultivated spontaneously. Virgil has Saturn journeying to Rome to preside over the fortunes of the City and its inhabitants. The Age of Saturn as well as other myths passed into the medieval world to mix, often in

5. Josef Pieper, *The End of Time: A Meditation on the Philosophy of History,* trans. Michael Bullock (New York: Pantheon, 1954), 13ff.

6. Frank E. Manuel, *Shapes of Philosophical History* (Stanford: Stanford Univ. Press, 1965), 82.

7. Isaiah Berlin, *Russian Thinkers,* ed. H. Hardy and A. Kelly (New York: Penguin, 1981), 22ff.

8. Cited by Frank Kermode, *The Sense of an Ending* (New York: Oxford Univ. Press, 1967), 167.

unsettling ways, with scriptural residues and to emerge later in state-of-nature theories and fantasies. The speculations of the ancient world, founded on a cyclical conception of time, were unable to construct a finished plot, which is the necessary ground for a philosophy of history.

A philosophy of history requires linear, non-repeatable time, a conception foreign to the classical mind. Because of this the superb accounts of Greek and Roman historians are chronicles not radically different from the less sophisticated works produced by the medievals. When Plato's philosopher descends from the contemplation of the Ideas to the play of shadows in the cave, he encounters the hyperkinetic phenomenal world which cannot, strictly speaking, be the object of knowledge. His universe is eternal, parsed out in endless cycles, a spectacular scenario in which individual things are of little importance. This is reflected in the ancient world's most sophisticated notion of deity, Aristotle's god, who, because of its perfection, knows only Itself.

Linear time was made possible through the biblical doctrine of creation. From Genesis it passed through the Prophets to Apocalyptic and is encountered full-blown in Daniel and the first-century *II Enoch*. The Jews had a more vigorous attitude towards ends, towards the future, than did the Greeks. This was inherited by Christianity, whose doctrine of the Incarnation linked creation indissolubly with temporal progression. Before the Christian era, Philo Judaeus in *De Aeternitate Mundi* criticized the notion of cycles and periodic destruction of the cosmos as the worst of profanities.[9] Throughout the Christian centuries Augustine's emotion-laden plaint that Christ will not again be crucified would be repeated in a multiplicity of variations.

From about the fourth century to the present the philosophy of history varies according to differing notions of the End. The End itself depends on the conception of the first principle or ultimate ground of reality. Yahweh Sabaoth replaces the Greek pantheon — both mythic and philosophic — and is Himself replaced by a surrogate, Providence, which, in turn, is ousted by Progress and its cult. The classical world picture, freighted with its eternal cycles, makes a brief appearance during the Re-

9. Cited by Manuel, *Shapes*, 11.

naissance, but it is not until Nietzsche that a major effort is made to reinstate the pagan cosmos by means of his theory of the Eternal Recurrence. Nietzsche's effort threatens to put an end to history by reabsorbing linear time into the cyclical whirl.

*   *   *

The present study begins with a prehistory of the philosophy of history, or in other words, with its origins. The doctrines of creation and Incarnation are the grounds of linear time. Time has a beginning, a midpoint — for Christians, the watershed of the Incarnation — and an End. Pagan recurrence is dismissed. Unlike Aristotle's Unmoved Mover, the biblical God is outpouring and overseeing, the Lord of History. From the prophetic books to the apocalyptic, of which Daniel is the paradigm, God's purposes are made patent in time. The question of the End perdures and is found with unique insistence in intertestamental Jewish apocalyptic. This passes into Revelation (The Apocalypse) and later uncanonical Christian eschatological and oracular works.

St. Augustine's *City of God (De Civitate Dei)* is arguably the best introduction to the philosophy of history. Historical themes merge with theological and philosophical insights to create a stunning panoramic mural. The struggle between two cities, the heavenly *(Civitas Dei)* and the earthly *(Civitas Terrena),* constitutes the ground of history, the lever which structures events and directs them to the End Times. Augustine's scheme provided the paradigm, the blueprint, for later thinkers, and is encountered, often in disguise, in such disparate minds as Vico and Marx. As Augustine discouraged chiliasm and extravagant speculation, it is at these points where departures from the main lines of his thought will be found.

At Augustine's suggestion, Orosius, a guest at Hippo, wrote a history[10] which, though it swerved from Augustine's path, was approved by a papal bull in 494 and was cited extensively throughout the Middle Ages. He followed the tradition of Origen and Bishop Eusebius, affirm-

---

10. Orosius, *The Seven Books of History Against the Pagans.* Karl Lowith, *Meaning in History* (Chicago: Univ. of Chicago Press, 1949), 249n.1.

ing that the Roman Empire was the providentially-established vehicle for the advancement of Christianity and that its post-incarnation history brings about the progressive realization of Divine Purpose, a view that was influential among late Roman Christians and would surface theoretically in the speculations of Otto von Freising and practically in the establishment of the Holy Roman Empire.

Medieval variations on the theme differed markedly. Those "Augustinians" who followed in the wake of Boethius took a different route than those "Augustinisants" who interpreted Augustine through the optics of Pseudo-Denis.[11] The latter would often begin at apocalyptic End Times and work backwards. Often, perhaps influenced by classical leftovers or intimations of Eden, history was interpreted as a fall from a golden age . . . now seen as vitiated by original sin. The reverse also was presented: history as a laborious ascent towards ever more perfect states under the aegis of the Divine Pedagogue.

Hildegard von Bingen, together with her contemporary Joachim of Fiore, was unique in that her speculations were anchored to visionary experiences which played a major role both in articulating her thought and expounding it. She viewed history as a progressive descent from the *tempus mulieribus* to the chaotic age of the gray wolf. On the contrary, Gerloh of St. Emmeran saw history as an upward spiral rising through progressive stages, following God's plan for the education of mankind. Otto von Freising, returning to the *City of God,* had the two cities growing together in a common society to which he gave the name of Christendom. In the Middle Ages there were many overlaps, as befits an age in which the *Dies Irae* coupled King David and the Sibyl as witnesses of the last days.

Departing from the path set by Augustine, Joachim of Fiore envisaged a higher state of human life situated between the present and the catastrophes of the End Times. Because of this he has been called the great anti-Augustinian in the development of Christian theory on the meaning of history. Abbot Joachim was the first to rigorously interpret history from

---

11. This distinction between 'Augustinians' and 'Augustinisants' is made by A. de Libera, "Augustin et Denys au moyen age," in *Saint Augustin,* ed. P. Ransom (Paris: L'Age d'Homme, 1988), 282.

the perspective of the Holy Trinity. Each Divine Person grounds a *status* or age. The ages move chronologically from the Age of the Father through that of the Son to the Age of the Holy Spirit, which is characterized by an elevated spirituality which will impregnate all areas of human endeavor.

Abbot Joachim placed a thought-egg in the Western consciousness that would have revolutionary consequences and is still to some extent present in the underbelly of the contemporary world. Only fairly recently Ernst Bloch called for a polis-less paraclitically permeated church that will call anew on the fraternal element in human life.[12] Although Bloch misunderstood Joachim and was probably influenced by later Joachite thought, his inspiration if not the letter proceeded from the Calabrian Abbot. It is a vibrant testimony to the ability of Joachim's thought to vault the centuries.

When Joachim's principal works fell into the hands of Franciscan *Zelanti* (Spirituals), his speculations began a wild career. It was initiated by Gerard of Borgo San Donnino's *Introduction to the Eternal Gospel (Introductorius in Evangelium Aeternum),* which contained these works or abstracts with commentary. St. Francis and the Franciscan order are here identified as the vehicles that would bring about that transformation of things which would characterize the third status, the Age of the Holy Spirit. Joachimists were followed by Joachites. Religious, social, and political agitation generated a tidal wave that reached the Age of Discovery, as evidenced by Columbus's *Libro de las Profecías.*[13] Secondary products of Joachite speculation, the Angel Pope and the Last World Emperor, became the longed-for purveyors of salvation. When religious and political aspirations failed to materialize, messianic expectations were shifted to the secular realm. Salvation would come from discovery, science, technology, and education.

During the Middle Ages, interesting and often subtle theories were

12. Ernst Bloch, *Man on His Own,* trans. E. B. Ashton (1959; New York: Herder & Herder, 1970), 60.

13. Christopher Columbus, *Libro de las Profecías,* trans. and commentary by Deláno West and August Kling (Gainesville: Univ. of Florida Press, 1992).

elaborated by Islamic and Jewish thinkers. Ibn Hazm and Ibn Khaldun show more than occasional flashes of insight. Jewish thinkers, nourished by the Torah and spurred on by Kabbalistic speculation, produced novel and often profound theories. Maimonides speculated on the time of the Messiah, though, like Thomas Aquinas, he discouraged eschatological prediction. Nachmanides, however, presents a wealth of ingenious prediction revolving about the messianic hope of a people crushed between Islam and Christianity. Both Maimonides and Nachmanides view the time of the Messiah as connected with Israel's liberation from the nations and the advent of a just world. Speculations such as these helped to spark the messianic pretensions of Sabbatai Zwi and entered into European history through the conjunction of Sabbateanism and the French Revolution in the person of Junius Frey.[14]

*   *   *

The modern world was adumbrated by Joachite speculation and the Latin Averroists, who advocated a theology-free enclave of speculation. This meld of fervid utopianism and desiccated reason combined to pave the way for the Renaissance. Aristotle's worldview, which rejected creation and advocated the eternal cycles, regained its popularity among the illustrated class. In fact, the Renaissance thinkers were slavishly dependent on often bizarre versions of ancient thought. From the viewpoint of the philosophy of history the Renaissance was no more than a hermetic interlude. Figures such as Pico della Mirandola and Giordano Bruno can be counted among the Magi of the period, announcing the advent of a utopia to be generated by means of esoteric experimentation. If the alchemist pretends to transform base metals into gold, social alchemy should be able to transmute a nasty and brutish society into a veritable paradise.

---

14. Junius Frey (a.k.a. Moses Dobrushka) belonged to a sect of radical Sabbatians, who called themselves *Maaminim* ('believers'), founded by Jacob Frank. His antinomian tendencies, an "unbounded political apocalypse," led him to the guillotine, together with Danton, in 1794. Gershom G. Scholem, *Major Trends in Jewish Mysticism* (New York: Schocken, 1967), 304f., 320, 421n.72.

From the utopia of Phaleas to those of Cabet and Hertzka and those spawned by the French Revolution, utopias have exercised a substantial influence on society and have contributed to the genesis of many philosophies of history when not ensconced in a cyclical worldview.

When historical speculation again took wings in the seventeenth century, it had lost much of its religious scaffolding due to a process of secularization, the tendency to preserve thoughts and habits of biblical origin after the atrophy of biblical faith. The awesome Deity of Scripture appears in the guise of an anemic surrogate: Providence. This is the case with Bishop Bossuet and Giambattista Vico. While Bossuet paints an impressive scenario with worn brushes inherited from the Augustinian tradition, marking a 'secret ordering' produced by the intertwining of *historia sacra* and *historia profana,* Vico elaborates a novel theory which, in its triadic structure, manifests a kinship with the speculations of Abbot Joachim. History moves in three stages following a determinate pattern which, albeit immutable and cyclical, more of a spiral than a circle, is nonetheless finite and directed by Providence. This is a rational civil theology of Divine Providence.

Hegel takes a great leap into profound depths, elaborating a theoretical web that issues from a center and extends to all of reality. He traces specific clusters of ideas which permeate an age, impinge on other ideas, and form vast symmetries. The center — the nodal point — is the Absolute of which the adequate concept is the Idea, the idea of freedom, which develops by means of a dialectical movement towards ultimate fulfillment. This dialectic operates in history when one culture, Greece for example, generates its opposite, Rome, and out of this thesis and antithesis, a synthesis is produced: the Christian world.

For Hegel, history is then a theodicy, a justification of God in time. However, the biblical ethos which pervades his thought is subservient to an omnipotent reason that constitutes reality and determines the *telos* of historical progression. Theology is assigned to the inferior level of imagination, which can only picture what reason can know. In a novel twist, history does not culminate in a distant future but rather in the present actuality of the Prussian state.

The cult of Progress, which is, in effect, Providence secularized, is already encountered in the thought of Adam Smith and Condorcet. Smith maintained that the liberation of appetite would bring about a continual expansion of productive forces without any foreseeable termination. Condorcet was the protégé of Turgot and under the influence of the views expressed in his address before the Sorbonne on the progressive advance of the human mind. Condorcet's *Esquisse* advocated unlimited progress by means of the cultivation of the sciences. This tome, ironically, was written in the shadow of the state-of-the-art guillotine while Condorcet was awaiting execution.

The anticlerical tilt of the *Esquisse* suggests that the Enlightenment's doctrine of Progress was produced by a secularization of the Christian theology of the Last Things. A treatise which exemplifies this trend employing religious terminology to convey secular concerns is Kant's "The Victory of the Good Principle over the Evil and the Establishment of the Kingdom of God on Earth" (1792). Kant dedicated a later treatise[15] to discuss three different views of progress, opting for *eudaemonism,* progression towards the better, maintaining that man's inclination to the good is demonstrated by his enthusiasm for the form of government established by the French Revolution.

However, insofar as the philosophy of history is concerned, the first prominent thinker to replace Providence by Progress was Auguste Comte. He believed that Joachim was one of his predecessors and that Christian belief in the superiority of the New Testament over the Old Testament foreshadowed the notion of human progress. Living at the center of French socialism as Saint-Simon's secretary, Comte found his theoretical basis in Hegel's Objective Spirit, which he employed to structure the often disparate and usually unrigorous ideas of the Physiocrats, a procedure which ultimately gave birth to sociology.

History, according to Comte, proceeds according to the 'great fundamental law' of Order and Progress, that passes through three non-repeatable stages culminating in the Positive or Scientific Age. Once this stage is arrived at, the three — mythological, metaphysical, positive — intermingle, but ultimately the vestiges of the prior stages will be erased and

15. Immanuel Kant, *Der Streit der Facultaten.*

the Positive will structure society. Comte joins Hegel in maintaining that the historical evolution of mankind is concentrated in the Christian West. However, to supply the agglutament that he believed was absent in modern society, Comte attempted to establish a religion of humanity, the 'Grand Être', patterned after medieval Christianity.

Positivism merged with socialism to produce mutations such as Proudhon. Progress hinges on the destruction of religion and its God, which hovers, vampire-like, over mankind to drain its lifeblood. Variations on the theme, many verging on the outrageous, were concocted and possessed no little importance. The cult of progress became an integral part of the public orthodoxy. It lost momentum only when the numbing horrors of the twentieth century forced a reconsideration of its status.

Perhaps the last great exponent of the gospel of progress is Karl Marx, albeit at a far remove from the effusions of the romantic socialism he abhorred. As Bakunin noted, Marx was triply authoritarian: as a Jew, as a German, and as a Hegelian. History is embodied in a succession of class struggles responding to a dialectic that moves towards ultimate human renovation. Strictly speaking, history has not yet begun! History will commence only after the proletarian revolution and the subsequent resolution of contradictions bring about the "realm of freedom." Like Hegel, Marx believed that history is a vehicle of progress, but he differed from Hegel on two major points. Its realization will take place in the future, not the present. Spirit cannot supersede nature, the immaterial cannot supersede the material. With Marx, history is reintegrated into nature, evolving according to immanent laws detached from any supernatural entity. While still preserving certain Augustinian traces on the subliminal level, Marx's speculations are frankly atheistic.

While the ideological heirs of the French Revolution surrendered to the lure of the gospel of progress, opponents of the Revolution, often adherents of the *ancien régime,* influenced by Augustine — or rather, by an idiosyncratic reading of his works — elaborated theories of inverse evolution. The French Traditionalists, headed by the Count de Maistre and de Bonald, were followed by the Spaniard, Donoso Cortés, who viewed history as a progressive decline furthered by the corruption of religion, the loss of authority, burgeoning technology, and the exacerbations of liberalism and socialism. On the horizon he envisioned a gigantic tyranny disguised as a humanitarian utopia. A parallel trend is encountered in the United States, reflected in the works of Orestes Brownson and present in Brooks Adams's *The Law of Civilization and Decay*. As Professor Molnar has suggested, Christianity, in desacralizing the cosmos and suppressing pagan mythology, opened the path towards a dehumanized world. As belief in the supernatural, which keeps the sacred alive, decreases, the pagan worldview which persists behind the Christian facade becomes increasingly present.[16]

*   *   *

With Friedrich Nietszche the philosophy of history arrives at an impasse, perhaps to be wrapped in a sheet and laid in a tomb. Through the theory of Eternal Recurrence linear time is again swallowed by the eternal cycles of classic Greek thought: *circulos vitiosus Deus*. *Zarathustra* was meant to be a counter-gospel grounded on the Will to Power that negates God, creation, and ethics, installing 'creative man' as the seat of authority. Out of the ruins of the 'last men', Nietzsche contemplates the rise of a superior man. Out of the rubble of the 'foul religion' that affirms death, he welcomes the advent of an earthly religion that affirms life. The 'death of God' opens the door to new possibilities while closing the gates to the philosophy of history. Although he spoke of the End of History as the definitive triumph of the masses, Nietszche's thought seems to preclude the genre or perhaps to predict a transvaluation.

In the wake of Nietszche, the barbarism of the twentieth century, prefaced by fin-de-siècle decadence, muted the excesses of romantic optimism. The notion of progress slipped to the status of a slogan. To many minds, history itself lost its meaning and plunged into the absurd. This feeling was adumbrated by Tolstoy who, in a letter to Nazariev, wrote that "history is nothing but a collection of fables and trifles, cluttered up with

16. Thomas Molnar, *The Pagan Temptation* (Grand Rapids: Eerdmans, 1987), 8-9, 44, 60, 79.

a mass of unnecessary figures and proper names."[17] It seems that the visions of prophets and the speculations of philosophers were being lost in the quagmire of mass culture with its Auschwitzes, gulags, and prevailing cacophony. In this unsettled world some thinkers returned to traditional eschatological themes, which enjoy pride of place in the works of Soloviev and Berdyaev and less speculative souls. Yeats, for example, believed the age would end in 1927.

*   *   *

A glance in the mirror seems to provide us with a general outline of the path taken by speculation on history. It begins by considering history as a canvas on which God's designs are inscribed. God is then replaced by Nature and its exigencies, Nature is replaced by Reason, and Reason replaced by Man, collective or individual. The canvas is then scrapped or borne away on the treadmill of the eternal universe. At the door, the most bizarre of all guests waits to be admitted: the Antichrist and his cohorts.

17. Cited by Berlin, *Russian Thinkers,* 31.

CHAPTER 1

Origins

The foundational charter of the philosophy of history is found in one biblical verse: "God, at the beginning of time, created heaven and earth" (Gen. 1:1-2). This text, as traditionally interpreted, shattered the pagan conception of an eternal universe parceled out in an infinity of cycles. That view was voiced by Berossus, the Babylonian astrologer, who maintained that the universe passes through a number of Great Years with each cosmic cycle reproducing that which had preceded it.[1] The doctrine of creation entailing linear time opened a vast horizon of novel events that took history beyond the limits of the ancient chroniclers. Even Herodotus, the father of history according to Cicero, in his nine books covering the struggle between Greeks and Persians, a superb epic in Homeric style, was nevertheless imprisoned in a circle.

The Bible has the unsettling penchant of universalizing the particular. Take the widespread myth of the flood, which is encountered in many cultures attached to the scheme of cosmic cycles. In Genesis the flood is incorporated into the history of mankind. All peoples are descended from Noah's three sons. Not only is the treadmill of cosmic cycles rejected, but mankind is accorded an unprecedented dignity: "Let us make man in our image to rule . . ." (Gen. 1:26). As man is made in the image of God and not of the cosmos, the ancient macrocosm/microcosm relation is

1. T. E. Glasson, *Greek Influence in Jewish Eschatology* (London: Nonesuch, 1961), 48.

scrapped. Creation is put at the service of man and man at the service of God.

The classic Hellenic order of priorities, a hierarchy descending from the Divine Cosmos to the gods, intermediary beings *(daimones)*, and finally to man, is thus rejected. In its place biblical thought establishes a hierarchy in which God reigns, is followed by man, and at a distant remove, the cosmos. God is a living being, not a principle; one, not a multiplicity; for Christians an *Unum* (one reality), not an *unus* (one person). The eternal cycles are abolished. Linear time has a beginning, middle, and an end. For Christians it has an apex — the Incarnation: to which and from which flow the tides of history.

The biblical mind views history as a drama which follows the Divine Script: "by the deliberate will and plan of God" (Acts 2:23). This merely echoes the prophets of the Old Testament, such as Amos, Isaiah, Jeremiah, and others, who were eschatologically minded, anticipating a future Kingdom of God ruled by a Messiah. This ideal future, quickened by nostalgia of past innocence, was firmly attached to the revelation of Yahweh. The New Testament begins on a note of fulfillment, reflected in St. Paul's dictum that the coming of Christ marks the fulfillment of history: "In this final age, He [God] has spoken to us in the Son whom he had made heir to the whole universe, and through whom he created all the orders of existence" (Heb. 1:2-3).

This enthronement of Christ as Lord of History was the culmination of a lengthy process in Wisdom literature (Eccles. 1:1; 3:1) by which Wisdom was, as it were, incorporated into the Godhead. It reached its zenith in the splendid hymn of praise to the Logos-God of the Gospel of John (John 1:1-18). Although the "new heaven" and the "new earth" proclaimed by Isaiah (65:17-25) set the stage for later apocalyptic text, Wisdom literature was prominent in preparing the way for the genre, of which Revelation (the Apocalypse) would be the Christian masterpiece.

The author of Revelation, presumably St. John, used traditional material drawn from several sources, reworking them in a novel manner. History melds with eschatology, reflecting the experienced tension between present reality and future hope: the establishment of God's kingdom on earth. The book of Revelation cannot be lodged within the framework of

Hellenic thought, as Hellenic thought cannot deal with either linear time or novelty. This is true of all apocalyptic literature, as it pretends to survey history as a whole and to do so, in Smithal's words, "knows about the goal . . . the consummation of history."[2]

For the apocalypticist to survey history as a whole is to view it as following some established plan, a plan which becomes the point of departure for the division of history into different ages, epochs, or stages. Sacred numbers such as four, seven, twelve, and seventy-two, connected with the seasons, signs of the zodiac, and so forth, were employed to establish the periods that made up history. Chronologies and divisions were considered to be of great value in tracing the fulfillment of Divine Purpose in time. Nevertheless, apocalyptic thought tends to look beyond history for its fulfillment. If the ultimate goal often resembles a utopia it would be what Mumford calls a "utopia of escape," one that leaves the world the way it is in expectation of a coming cataclysmic judgment.[3]

The surviving Jewish and Christian apocalypses date from before 200 BC to somewhat after 200 AD, from the book of Daniel to the *Sibylline Oracles*. These were accompanied by the so-called "little apocalypses" of the Gospels (Mark 13; Matt. 24–25; Luke 21). With the passage of time apocalyptic literature waned. The original emphasis on history was lost and the genre faded in the process of finding expression in scriptural commentaries and theological treatises. Historical patterns are evident in the Epistle of Barnabas, in which the 'cosmic week' developed an interpretation of world history that looks forward to the Second Coming — when the time of the 'Wicked One' will be destroyed.[4]

Jewish apocalyptic literature burgeoned with the revival of Jewish nationalism during the struggle of the Maccabees against Antiochus Epiphanes. After 70 AD, as apocalyptic thought began to lose ground in mainstream Judaism, it entered Christianity when the Septuagint translation of the Old Testament, which contained apocalyptic works, was adopted. Christians proceeded to produce new writings such as the Apoc-

2. Walter Schmithals, *The Apocalyptic Movement,* trans. John E. Steeley (Nashville: Abingdon Press, 1975), 18.

3. Lewis Mumford, *The Story of Utopias* (New York: Boni and Liveright, 1928), 15.

4. Epistle of Barnabas 15:4-5.

alypse of Peter and the Shepherd of Hermas. Apocalyptic thinking continued to exercise considerable influence until it was rejected by Judaism and muted within Christianity.

The paradigm had been provided by the book of Daniel, in which themes are presented in luminous, metallic colors. The monstrous figure (Dan. 2:7) composed of four metals gave rise to a multiplicity of interpretations. But more to the point is the division of history from the Babylonian captivity onwards into seventy weeks[5] of years on the basis of the prophecy of Jeremiah (25:11-12; 29:10). These are in turn divided into three periods of seven weeks, sixty-two weeks, and one week, after which the end will come.

Following in the wake of Daniel, I Enoch proceeds to divide history into ten weeks, seven of which have already passed. History fast approaches the tenth and final week, that of the last judgment, to be followed by a paradaisical age. The Book of Jubilees divides history into jubilee periods of forty-nine years, each of which is subdivided into seven weeks of years. Another division that gained acceptance in the first century was triadic. First is the period of chaos, the 'tohu wa-bohu' (without form and void) of Gen. 1:2; then that of the Torah, commencing with the Mount Sinai revelation; finally, the time of the Messiah.[6] With suitable adjustments this schema would pass into Christian theological speculation.

Apocalyptic thought is pessimistic in that it suggests that there is no salvation in this eon, that the world must be transcended. As the world has been corrupted through its capitulation to the powers of evil it would have to be, in some way, renewed, even by means of its destruction. Because of this the old and new ages are as distinct as God and Satan, light and darkness, life and death. 4 Esdras 7:50 states it quite clearly: "the

---

5. "A socially constructed unit of time whose duration is intermediate between the astronomical units of day and lunar month. In various cultures weeks of four, five, six, seven, eight, ten, or fifteen days have been known to exist . . . the seven day week is probably of Israelite origin. . . . Even the sectarian calendars of Jub. 6:29-38, Enoch 72–75 and Qumran . . . left the seven-day week intact." B. E. Shafer, "Week," *The Interpreter's Dictionary of the Bible* (Nashville: Abingdon Press, 1976), Supp. Vol., p. 946.

6. D. S. Russell, *The Method and Language of Jewish Apocalyptic* (1964; Philadelphia: Westminster, 1976), 53ff.

Most High has made, not one age but two."[7] This dichotomy will be inte-
grated into the course of a common history by later speculation. However,
it will be carried over to the anthropological realm, as evidenced by a multiplicity of biblical texts, and later superbly orchestrated by St. Augustine
in the *City of God.*

The contrast between two types of people is given significant importance in apocalyptic literature. In 1 Enoch God separates the spirits of the
"children of light" from those of the "children of darkness." The Apocalypse of Abraham has the patriarch contemplating a world divided into
two camps: on the right, God's people; on the left, the heathen. More dramatic, Qumran's Rule for the Final War describes the final apocalyptic
battle between the "sons of light" and the "sons of darkness," which puts
an end to the present era and opens the door to the kingdom. The docu-
ment is surprisingly specific. Each side will win three battles. Then God
will intervene, ensuring the victory of the "sons of light."[8]

The progression, which begins in Genesis, passes through the Prophets,
wisdom and apocalyptic literature, peaks with Revelation and the
Johannine Gospel, and enters the future in a disfigured and unexpected
manner. As Zubiri has indicated, at the instant that the Logos is identified
as Christ, speculation launches on a wild career in which the Logos, the essence of God, ends as the essence of man.[9] Moreover, the utopian character
of apocalyptic possessed the power to influence the secular realm to the
point of creating novel social structures as illustrated, prior to Christianity,
by the Qumran community. The trend, which began in intertestamental
pseudepigrapha and writings such as Enoch and Jubilees, gains force in
Revelation and manifests itself on the social level throughout the course of
history in popular movements and pseudomessiahs such as Konrad
Schmid, Bernt Rothmann, and Abiezer Coppe.[10]

The West spawned many heirs of apocalyptic thought, among whom
Marx can be numbered as one of the most prominent. He also actualizes

7. Cited by Smithals, *Apocalyptic Movement,* 40, 81, 109.
8. Russell, *Method and Language,* 45.
9. Xavier Zubiri, *Naturaleza, Historia, Dios* (Madrid: Editoria Nacional, 1963), 229.
10. Cf. Norman Cohn, *The Pursuit of the Millennium* (Fairlawn: Essential Books, 1957).

the idea of the domain of evil in history, of the ultimate victory of the good, and of the immanent inbreaking of the messianic kingdom at the end of history.[11]

*   *   *

The opposition of Christianity to paganism may be seen with clarity in their respective approaches to history. Plotinus depicts historical events as incidents in a play, placing them in sharp contrast with authentic life, that of interiority, the drama of the return of the soul to God.[12] Before him, Plato, in the *Phaedrus,* ranked gymnastics higher than prophecy.[13] Aristotle, when he contemplated the future, saw only a whirl of events and things repeating themselves endlessly.[14]

The notions of deity are radically different. When Plato mentions 'god' as he does at the inception of the *Laws*[15] or at the end of the *Apology,*[16] he is simply invoking the popular deity, the 'god' of the citizens of Athens. This is rhetoric, not philosophy or theology. Aristotle's god is not a creator. It relates to the physical world only as final cause of motion and desire. A true aristocrat, this Unmoved Mover cannot mix in human or galactic affairs from its self-contained perch.[17]

This is reflected in the political sphere as well. Plato elaborates his utopia in the *Republic* under the guidance of philosophy, leaving matters of praxis to the *Statesman* and the *Laws,* in which philosophy plays no role. The *Republic* cannot be actualized, cannot be constructed in the material world, though as a paradigm it can effect the improvement of exist-

---

11. Smithals, *Apocalyptic Movement,* 237, 243ff.

12. Plotinus, *Enneads* 3, 2.

13. Plato, *Phaedrus* 246-57. Ten thousand years comprise one world period or cycle. The *Statesman* indicates that world periods alternate with each other in a manner similar to that advanced by Empedocles (268e ff.). See Paul Friedlander, *Plato,* trans. Hans Meyeroff (Princeton: Princeton Univ. Press, 1969), 1:202ff.

14. Aristotle, *On Generation and Corruption* 336b28-33; 337al; 338a16-18; 338b8-9 et al.

15. Plato, *Laws* 624a.

16. Plato, *Apology* 42a.

17. Aristotle, *Metaphysics* 1074b15-34 et al.

ing politics. Politics becomes a movement either of approximation or withdrawal from the paradigm.

Christianity was originally an underclass religion and according to its critics remained so even after Constantine. Even in Augustine's day, the academies and the libraries were in the hands of pagans and would remain so for an additional, albeit brief, period. It was imperative for Christians to come to terms with classical thought. This awareness matured only slowly among Christians, who strongly resisted accepting the value of worldly knowledge. St. Paul was himself ambivalent. The censures found in Colossians (2:8-9) are balanced, at least to some extent, by the Areopagus discourse (Acts 17:22-35). Others, such as Tertullian, were adamant: Christ's wisdom is the only true wisdom! Worldly knowledge is superfluous, perhaps even diabolical, and should be rejected.

Clement of Alexandria broadcast a contrary view, maintaining that philosophy prepared the way for the gospel among the Gentiles in a manner analogous to that by which the Torah did the Jews. Though hardly a full-fledged endorsement — in the banquet of wisdom, pagan knowledge is merely the dessert — it opened the door to a greater appreciation of Greco-Roman thought, without which the theological and philosophical exploits of the following centuries would have been impossible. This is no less true of the relatively minor enclave of the theology/philosophy of history. It was a time of crisis, when everything is a bit everything, and such a view makes a turnabout possible. In any case, Augustine's "spiolare Aegyptos" was to turn the tide, and classical thought would assume its position of *ancilla theologiae* until the upsets of the late medieval period.

Augustine reasoned that as God is Truth and all truth belongs to him, it is the legitimate patrimony of the Christian and should be considered as such. This was not the end of the matter. The conflict between biblical and pagan wisdom became a stormy intramural affair that grew especially violent when their antithetical cosmologies rose to the surface. Insofar as speculation regarding history is concerned, Augustine's interpretation held pride of place until modernity. The mathematization of nature, characteristic of the new science, is singularly ahistorical. When, in June 1553, the seventy-year-old Galileo knelt in front of the Tribunal of the

Inquisition and muttered the apocryphal *"E pur si move"* we encounter the final break between medieval faith and scientific rationalism, a break which would have noteworthy consequences for the philosophy of history.

The progressive appropriation of the Earthly City by the Heavenly City is implicit in the Our Father's "thy will be done on earth as it is in heaven." This principle, which aimed at constituting an earthly society structured by the norms of the heavenly court (nicely exemplified by the fifth book of Augustine's *De civitate Dei*), fell victim to the progressive secularization that displaced God from the center of reality. This hardening of the religious arteries began on a large scale in the Renaissance, was furthered by the Reformation, continued during the Enlightenment, was accelerated by the French Revolution, and perhaps is completed in the dehumanized "culture" that today threatens the very basis of civilization. Philosophy of history, severed from its contrapuntal relation[18] to theology, might well be condemned to wander aimlessly in the void or simply to wilt on the stalk. There is, nevertheless, always the possibility that, as the poet writes:

This air will crystallize
into some marvelous event.[19]

18. See Josef Pieper, *The End of Time: A Meditation on the History of Philosophy,* trans. Michael Bullock (New York: Pantheon, 1954), 18.

19. Charles Williams, "The Chaste Wanton." Cited by Alice Mary Hadfield, *Charles Williams* (New York: Oxford Univ. Press, 1983), 81.

CHAPTER 2

St. Augustine

It is hardly arbitrary to begin this study of the philosophy of history with St. Augustine in spite of difficulties and dissenting opinions: the Middle Ages was dominated by his thought. After the Renaissance his influence was present in Bossuet, Vico and beyond, casting its shadow over Hegel and Marx while inspiring a somewhat crabbed discipleship in the French Traditionalists and Donoso Cortés. Harnack called *De civitate Dei* (*The City of God*) Augustine's *Divine Comedy,* a nice though ambivalent compliment. Like Dante's masterpiece it raises many questions. Does the *City of God* present a philosophy of history, a theology of history, a historical hermeneutic,[1] or none of the three?[2] It remains a hotly debated issue. Ancillary to these questions are others: if the work is, in fact, a philosophy or a theology of history, is it full-blown or only in a larval stage? Is it a serious intellectual discipline . . . a science?

Augustine left a blueprint replete with unexplored possibilities, a transcendent vision brought down to earth by a conception of time inherited from Scripture. He created a scenario that contains the course of events

1. Supporters of the first view (philosophy of history) include Lowith, Figgis, Padovani, and Sciacca; of the second (theology of history), Marrou and Copleston; of the third (historical hermeneutic), J. Moran. For complete data, refer to the bibliography. See Jean Danielou, "Philosophie ou Theologie de l'histoire." *Dieu Vivant* 19 (1951).

2. O'Meara, Chadwick, Knowles, and Ratzinger argue that Augustine does not present, strictly speaking, a philosophy of history and opt for other interpretations.

and provides a foundation for their development. This is the original pattern, formed in an age of catastrophe, that generated a host of variations and permutations down through the ages. The eternal cosmos with its infinite cycles is discarded along with the other characteristics of the pagan worldview. Linear time is established. This is done, as it were, in passing, while presenting a lengthy apologia for Christianity that undermines the foundations of paganism.

His reasoning is simple in its profundity. All society is grounded on a common love, "a multitude of rational beings united by common agreement on the objects of their love."[3] There exist two basic, albeit contrary, loves. The love of the immutable and infinite good — God — is one; the love of finite, mutable goods — the other. Each love excludes the contrary. Each love constitutes a 'city' or society, what Brown nicely describes as a "pyramid of loyalty."[4] These two cities existed even prior to the creation of mankind in the ranks of the faithful and rebellious angels. The human cities arise with the creation of Adam and are symbolized by Jerusalem and Babylon, the heavenly and earthly societies.

Though Adam contained the elements of the two societies in his own person, these inner dispositions become explicit only with Cain and Abel. The Bible itself dwells on the antitheses between the wheat and the tares, the new and the old man, and the outer and inner self, made explicit by St. Paul in vivid colors.[5] Augustine delights in contrasting the two cities. The earthly city lives by the standard of the flesh — he cites the catalogue of vices given in Galatians 5:19-21; the heavenly city by the standard of the spirit. Each individual is able to choose to live either according to God's standard or those of the flesh, reducible to self-will, "living by rule of self,"[6] the prime characteristic of the earthly city.

Two loves create two cities: the earthly city is formed by self-love to the contempt of God; the heavenly city by love of God to the contempt of self.[7]

3. Augustine, *De civitate Dei* 19, 24.
4. Peter Brown, *Augustine of Hippo* (Berkeley: Univ. of California Press, 1969), 324.
5. Ephesians 2:19; Philippians 3:20.
6. Augustine, *De civitate Dei* 14, 3.
7. Augustine, *De civitate Dei* 14, 28.

Augustine, in the *Confessions,* had formulated the principle *"amor meus, pondus meum."*[8] In the *City of God* this principle is projected outwards to become a social norm. Not only does the individual gravitate toward what he loves, in a sense becoming it, but love also binds him together with others. It acts as a social adhesive, binding men together to constitute a city, either of God or of Man, heavenly or earthly. The history of humanity is simply the period of development *(excursus)* of these two cities.[9]

Each city has a *telos,* a goal, an end. The earthly city moves towards supreme evil, identified with eternal death by Augustine. The heavenly city moves towards supreme good, eternal life. The initial act of the cosmic drama witnesses the foundation of the two cities, the last their salvation or damnation, moving from creation to the End Times as depicted in Revelation and interpreted by Christian exegesis. Between these two poles history takes place, an interim period regulated by the ebb and flow of the struggle between the two cities. Between the light of creation and the obscurity of the End Times the heavenly city on earth weaves, as a barque, through the troubled waters of centuries, its ultimate victory experienced at present only in hope.

The citizens of the earthly city are very much at home in the world; they rest content with temporal happiness. Cain founded a city and Scripture testifies to the productivity of his descendants.[10] Abel was a pilgrim in the world as is the heavenly city in the person of its citizens.[11] Peter Brown speaks of the citizens of the heavenly city as resident aliens,[12] an apposite designation as they belong to a society that grows in the shade of the earthly city and is, in fact, its positive double.[13] Augustine speaks of pilgrims in a foreign land, who, albeit in captivity, make use of those things necessary for life, obeying those laws of the earthly city designed to further the common good. In these essentials a 'harmony' is

8. Augustine, *Confessions* 13, 9.
9. Augustine, *De civitate Dei* 15, 1.
10. Genesis 17:23f.
11. Augustine, *De civitate Dei* 15, 1; 15, 4 et al.
12. Brown, *Augustine,* 313-29.
13. Augustine, *De civitate Dei* 18, 1; 18, 47.

preserved.[14] This recalls the words of the *Letter to Diognetus:* "They live in their own countries but are aliens . . . every foreign land is their country, and every country is foreign to them."[15]

The earthly city is bonded together by "a sort of fellowship based on a common nature" and aspires to peace under law.[16] Both cities aspire to peace even by means of war. But the peace of final happiness is granted only to the City of God: "the name of the city itself has a mystic significance, for 'Jerusalem' . . . means 'vision of peace.'"[17] This apparent separation between the two cities is not found during their historical existence as here they are found intermixed. Their frontiers merge. Though Augustine does speak of the church as the City of God on pilgrimage,[18] they are not identified. This allows for human error while increasing the possibility of clashes between the two societies.

These clashes will usually arise in the religious domain: the church as imperfect representative of the *Civitas Dei* cannot tolerate laws that set up false gods. At this point, Augustine indicates, it is obliged to become a "burdensome nuisance" until it prevails by means of Divine Aid and, on the level of political praxis, "the terror inspired by her numbers."[19] The religious idealist marches in unison with the pragmatic tactician. Once assured of orthodox worship the citizens of the heavenly city are able to lead a life of righteousness and employ the peace of the terrestrial city to their advantage.

Augustine comes to identify the Beast of the Apocalypse with the ungodly city and, following the text of Revelation, credits the final defeat of the Antichrist to Jesus Christ himself, present in person.[20] He paints an impressive, often chilling, picture of the two cities engaged in a spiritual struggle, in which the events that make up history ride like whitecaps on a choppy sea, propelled by powerful underlying currents.

---

14. Augustine, *De civitate Dei* 19, 17; 19, 26.

15. *Epist. ad Diognetum* 5.5. Cited by E. R. Dodds, *Pagan and Christian in an Age of Anxiety* (Cambridge: Cambridge Univ. Press, 1965), 20.

16. Augustine, *De civitate Dei* 18, 2; 19, 14.

17. Augustine, *De civitate Dei* 19, 11. Comparison of the two notions of peace, 19, 17.

18. Augustine, *De civitate Dei* 13, 16.

19. Augustine, *De civitate Dei* 19, 17; 19, 26.

20. Augustine, *De civitate Dei* 18, 53; 20, 14.

The occasion that provoked the writing of *De civitate Dei* was ostensibly the sack of Rome by the Christian Goths under Alaric on August 24, 410. The event had a tremendous effect on most contemporaries. A foreign enemy had violated the 'City' after eight centuries of sanctuary. To some it appeared that the very foundations of order and civilization were toppling. Centuries later, something of the same mood was produced by Nietzsche's proclamation of the death of God. The center does not hold! St. Jerome reacted predictably. He stopped dictating and lamented that the human race had perished with Rome, even though Orosius reported that the damage to the City was not serious.

To the pagans, the conservatives of the day, who delighted using Christians as a whipping boy,[21] this was the proverbial last straw. They took the occasion to increase their attacks against opponents they disdained and feared, dredging up anti-Christian tracts and arguments. Pagan distaste, from a religious perspective, was not only focused on the many measures which had been taken to curb the public expression of the ancient rite, but on those Christian beliefs, such as the resurrection of the body, which they found particularly objectionable. Celsus had called it "revolting and impossible" while the great Plotinus observed that the true resurrection is not *with* the body but *from* the body.[22]

The sack of Rome, if his invective against Rome can be taken literally, could not have seriously affected Augustine. If empires are really only robbery on a large scale, mournful lament would be out of place. Seen in retrospect, it may be interpreted as the death rattle of the Roman Empire. Yet Augustine believed that Rome would perdure. He had witnessed the conflict between Church and Rome at first hand, arriving in Milan only a few days after the culmination of the dispute between Symmachus, Prefect of Rome, his own patron, and St. Ambrose, the Bishop of Milan. The Christian poet, Prudentius, describes how the Senate formally banished Jupiter and the other pagan deities while enshrining the God of the Bible.[23]

---

21. All calamities, even drought, were blamed on the Christians. Augustine, *De civitate Dei* 2, 3.

22. Origen, *Contra Celsus* 5, 14; Plotinus, *Enneads* 3, 6, 6.

23. John O'Meara, introduction to Augustine, *City of God,* trans. Henry Bettenson (1967; London: Penguin, 1984), xii.

The collapse of paganism triggered a strong reaction from the educated aristocracy and the peasantry. Marcellinus raised the question in a letter to Augustine of 412. Two letters from Augustine in reply announce the themes presented in the *City of God*.[24] Other works adumbrated it.[25] The title itself was taken from the Psalter (86:3), accentuating its religious tilt. The *tempora Christiana,* the Christian age, is a reality wending its way to a promising though uncertain future. Whatever vicissitudes interrupt its progress, the solidarity between the heavenly city triumphant and its temporal presence assures it of ultimate victory.

Aside from their biblical antecedents the two "cities" had a pagan counterpart in the traditional pagan antithesis between the celestial world and the terrestrial postulated by the ancient astronomers that reappears in Cicero, Seneca, and Celsus.[26] Close at hand is Tyconius the Donatist, a veritable contemporary who discusses the two cities in his commentary on Revelation, a work with which Augustine was familiar. Moreover, Augustine's nine-year association with the Manichees must have made him sensitive to the interplay of light and darkness, good and evil, which they portrayed so dramatically. In an age of syncretism, this spectacular manifestation of Gnosticism must have weighed heavily on his imagination. Elements of differing sizes came together in the crucible of Augustine's mind to produce the impressive ocean-sea of the *City of God*.

Henry Chadwick notes that the title was chosen so as to offer a conscious contrast to the *Republics* of Plato and Cicero.[27] The voluminous work in twenty-two books took Augustine thirteen years, roughly from the age of fifty-nine to that of seventy-two. The first five books deal with the polytheists who believed that the old gods protected Roman interests. The next five (6-10) are addressed to those Neoplatonists who accepted the polytheistic tradition as a path to purification. The remaining twelve books — including the nineteenth dedicated to the overlapping values of the two cities — present Augustine's most profound speculations: four

24. Augustine, *Epist.* 137, 138.
25. O'Meara, in Augustine, *City of God,* xv-xix.
26. Refer to E. R. Dodds, *Pagan and Christian,* 7-8.
27. Henry Chadwick, *Augustine* (Oxford: Oxford Univ. Press, 1986), 97.

(11-14) deal with the origin of the two cities, four (15-18) with their development in the past, and four (19-22) with their ultimate destinies.

If Augustine's notion of the City of God is lacking in precision — the best that can be said is the church represents it rather by symbol than by identification[28] — his attitude to Rome was clearly ambivalent. On the one hand, Rome represents the earthly city caught in the grip of malevolent forces. On the other, it plays a part in the providential dissemination of Christianity. His demythologization of the pagan *mundus* scored Rome. It is given no special status. Far different from his guest and sometime disciple Orosius, who, in his *Historia adv. Paganos,* followed in the steps of Eusebius and stressed the providential role of the Roman Empire, Augustine has Christianity, the ultimate world religion, paralleled by Rome, the ultimate world state, which, according to his interpretation of Daniel,[29] will perdure until the coming of Antichrist. This conception, as Markus has indicated, would exercise a great influence on Christian thought, even after the disasters of the early fifth century.[30]

Although E. R. Dodds may be right in contending that in actual history there are no 'periods' or 'ages' but rather a smooth-flowing continuum,[31] a thinker is obliged to effect a *prise de distance,* and from this perch to subject the flow to scrutiny. Augustine inherits two divisions that he accepts, one of three periods, one of seven. They are related to his pivotal conception of the two cities somewhat as plays within a play. *Hamlet* comes to mind. The first has Rabbinic roots. During the first period (without the Law), there was no attempt to oppose the lure of the world. During the second (under the Law), an unsuccessful attempt was made to do so, followed by the third (the era of grace), when victory over the

28. See John N. Figgis, *The Political Aspects of St. Augustine's 'City of God'* (London: Longmans, Green, 1921), 51. However, Harnack maintained that "the empirical Catholic Church is also the Kingdom of God." *History of Dogma,* trans. from the third German edition by Neil Buchanan (New York: Dover, 1968), 5:151.

29. Daniel 2:7. The four metals of the monstrous figure (head of gold, breast of silver, belly and thighs of brass, legs of iron, feet of clay) were commonly interpreted as four kingdoms, Rome being the fourth.

30. R. A. Markus, *History and Society in the Theology of St. Augustine* (1970; Cambridge: Cambridge Univ. Press, 1988), 51.

31. Dodds, *Pagan and Christian,* 3.

mundus is finally achieved. This schema was well-known and would be used even by innovators such as Joachim of Fiore.

The second schema was adapted from Christian sources such as Hippolytus of Rome, who maintained that history follows the pattern of the six days of creation. This would later pass on to the Middle Ages and be reflected in the Hexaemeron genre, markedly in that of St. Bonaventure.[32] This schema is divided into six ages: (1) Adam to Noah: the *infancy* of mankind which ends with the Flood; (2) Noah to Abraham: the *childhood* of mankind which witnesses the confusion of tongues; (3) Abraham to David: the *youth* of mankind, when the Law is given and the divine promises resonate more clearly; (4) David to the Babylonian captivity: *manhood,* the epoch of kings and prophets; (5) the Babylonian captivity to Christ: *maturity,* when prophecy ceases and, in spite of the rebuilding of the Temple, Israel is humbled; (6) Christ to the EndTime: *old age,* the period of grace, struggle, and final victory. This leads to the Eternal Sabbath when time will be swallowed in eternity.[33]

Augustine refers to scriptural narratives which refer to future events as *prophetica historia.*[34] This would seem to entail that "sacred history" is the basis of his philosophy of history and that world history is judged according to its exigencies. However, there is both a move from the history of Israel to Christ and a further movement by which the effects of the Incarnation radiate throughout the world. St. Athanasius put it forcefully: "He has been manifested in a human body for this reason only. . . . The renewal of creation has been wrought by the self-same Word who made it in the beginning."[35] It would seem that redeemed time has displaced secular time.

After the Incarnation the two cities are intertwined in the *Saeculum.*[36]

32. Cf. Joseph Ratzinger, *The Theology of History in St. Bonaventure* (Chicago: Franciscan Herald Press, 1971).

33. Augustine, *De Gen. contra Man.* 23, 25-24, 42.

34. Augustine, *De civitate Dei* 16, 2-3.

35. Athanasius, *On the Incarnation,* introduction by C. S. Lewis. Translated and edited by a religious of C.S.M.N. (1944; Crestwood: St. Vladimir's Orthodox Theological Seminary, 1993), #9, p. 35.

36. Refer to Markus, *History and Society,* 53f., 63n.3.

St. Augustine

Instead of concluding, as does Markus, that the history of the church is no longer part of sacred history, it may be suggested that all of history becomes incorporated into sacred history insofar as the new life of the second creation radiates through it. Instead of a secularization of history[37] a good argument can be made that, in a sense, the reverse holds true. All history becomes sacred history. Once the cyclical treadmill of the pagans is rejected, history moves in a straight line.[38]

Augustine was not a system-builder. He did not set out to elaborate a philosophy of history. Whatever the influence of Plotinus, and it was great, Augustine could not follow in his ahistorical tracks simply because the Incarnation marks the entrance of God into history, the field of Christ's mission. From a purely formal scholastic point of view it is possible to fault Augustine and deny that he should be considered a philosopher of history. One of the proponents of this view is Professor Ratzinger.[39] But this criterion is both too narrow and too brittle. Perhaps Figgis was on the mark when he stated that "no one who takes the Incarnation seriously can avoid some kind of philosophy of history,"[40] a statement that possesses unexplored possibilities.

Well over a millennium after Augustine's death, Auguste Comte, positivist and philosopher of history, observed that to consider the "law of Christ" superior to the "law of Moses" already entails a notion of progress. Providence also enters the picture. Progress and providence will have a lengthy career in historical speculation even after Augustine's worldview is largely rejected and the scriptural God domesticated or forgotten. Augustine considered that providence guides all things *ab angelo ad vermiculum,* from the angel to the worm,[41] and is the key to the solution of all conflicts and enigmas. Providence operates in the realm of nature as well as in society and history. It is not without importance that

37. Markus, *History and Society,* 133.
38. Augustine, *De civitate Dei* 12, 13-14.
39. Ratzinger, *Theology of History,* 76. "History is a flow of individual events; that which is common or general in these events is not known. Consequently, there can be no real sense of history; for science treats precisely the universal."
40. Figgis, *Political Aspects,* 34.
41. Augustine, *De div. quaest.* 83, q. 53, 2.

Varro, Augustine's authority on mythology, held providence in high esteem.

From the perspective of the "sublime ordering" dictated by providence, history can be seen as an "ineffable poem" which enchants by its admirable beauty.[42] The 'Platonists' may claim to touch eternity in their noetic ascents, but they were stymied by the lower world, "the closewoven sequence of centuries," the process by which humanity courses onward like a vast river, towards the goal of which they were ignorant.[43] Augustine approaches the problem delicately. Although history is subsumed under this-worldly knowledge *(scientia)* it derives its importance from its relation to wisdom *(sapientia)* just as the contingent derives its importance — and being — from the eternal. Augustine is able to plot the course of the river in broad strokes. World history, closely considered, is one episode in the time-process.

As Lowith stated, "Augustine was able to construct universal history as one purposeful *procursus* from beginning to end, without an intermediate millennium."[44] All of history is part of a scheme so vast the contours are scarcely visible. Augustine was gifted with a privileged insight into the nature of time, an extension of his magisterial discussion in the *Confessions*.[45] He was not an academic thinker marking out his territory but a visionary captivated by those things that leave the professional cold. Hugo Rahner has suggested, following a long tradition, that history is a "divine comedy." Augustine himself declared that this life is nothing but a comedy of the human race,[46] a radically contingent comedy.

Augustine insisted that when God created the world he created time.[47] This world, like the things that comprise it, responds to a "seminal reason" or pattern that transcends the powers of the human mind. The indi-

---

42. Augustine, *De civitate Dei* 11, 18; *Epist.* 138, 1, 5, et al.

43. Augustine, *De Trinitate* 4, 26, 21.

44. Karl Lowith, *Meaning in History* (Chicago: Univ. of Chicago Press, 1949), 167.

45. Augustine, *Confessions,* book 11.

46. Augustine, *Enarr. ad Ps.* 127. As mentioned previously, Porphyry calls history a "tragi-comedy," *Ad Marc.* 2. Plato refers to men and women as "puppets" since they possess only a small portion of reality. *Laws* 804b, 644d-e.

47. Augustine, *Confessions* 11, 13.

vidual soul strives to ascend to spiritual vision by several stages, moving from the carnal to the spiritual, from the temporal to the eternal, until the divine image is perfected.[48] The cosmos represented by humanity, adrift in time, must also run a similar course. But this should not be understood as a preordained march to a perfected world, to a utopia. Humanity is subject to all the tragedies, failures, and defeats that are encountered in the life of an individual . . . and perhaps more. The great poem of history is humanity's response to divine improvisation. It is comparable to the Psalter, a continuous act of praise to God.

The City of God mentions only two empires, the Assyrian and the Roman, perhaps foreshadowing Hegel's view that meaningful history moves from east to west. Up to the Incarnation it is true that "secular" and "sacred" history march to the beat of different drummers. We have made a case that this is not so after Christ's birth. An intriguing solution was given by a later "Augustinisant," Otto von Freising, in his *History of the Two Cities*. He contends that two separate historical shapes should be used: cyclism for profane history, meaningful progression for sacred history.[49] This may be seen as a pointer towards later philosophies of history and as such it deserves mention.

However, his answer limps insofar as the question at hand is concerned. Cyclism has suffered a metamorphosis. It has to some extent been baptized and, after the Incarnation, is subsumed under the meaningful progression of "sacred history" and subject to its exigencies. We should recall, with Augustine, that:[50]

> The ungodly will walk in a circle, not because their life is going to come round again in the course of those revolutions which they believe in, but because the way of their error, the way of false doctrine, goes around in circles.

48. Augustine, *De Trinitate* 15, 17, 23.

49. Frank E. Manuel, *Shapes of Philosophical History* (Stanford: Stanford Univ. Press, 1965), 33.

50. Augustine, *De civitate Dei* 12, 14. Augustine is citing Psalm 12:9 as found in the Latin versions derived from the Septuagint. The NEB reads "the wicked flaunt themselves on every side."

In a bizarre analog to Augustine's two societies, though perhaps borrowed from it, Professor Leo Strauss has urged that Western history reflects, "we could almost say *is*," the conflict between the biblical and the philosophic notions of the good life. This conflict, albeit "unsolvable," is the "secret" of the vitality of Western civilization.[51] He contrasts the "one thing needful" proclaimed by the Bible, "a life of obedient love," and that put forward by Greek philosophy, "a life of autonomous understanding."[52] As Strauss obviously favors the second we experience the strange sensation of facing a mirror image of Augustine's two cities. This testifies to the persistence of Augustine's style of thought, tone of argument, and underlying imagery. However, it is dubious that Augustine would have endorsed the view that the struggle between the earthly and the heavenly cities is not only the lever which controls history but also the prod for its advancement.

Whether or not Augustine is credited with elaborating a full-blown philosophy of history, there is little doubt that he deposited a seed in the psyche of the West that would prove to be abundantly fruitful for well over fifteen centuries. By discarding the eternal cosmos, postulating linear time, and making thematically explicit what is implicit in Scripture, Augustine opened the door to the philosophy of history. His insight into history passed over into other areas of his thought with often surprising consequences. In the *Confessions* he wrote what could, without exaggeration, be called a proto-autobiography, a genre unknown to the ancient world. The portraits of the classic writers (even that of the Christian Eusebius) were static. They still were under the influence of a cyclic conception of time that did not allow for novelty, for development.

Insofar as hermeneutics is concerned, Beryl Smalley indicates that Augustine gave the 'letter' a concrete reality which it had not heretofore possessed. She remarks that "the narrative of Scripture is fitted into a philosophy of history based on the Incarnation."[53] But it is in the philosophy

---

51. Leo Strauss, "Progress or Return? The Contemporary Crisis in Western Civilization," in *An Introduction to Political Philosophy: Ten Essays by Leo Strauss,* ed. Hilail Gilden (1975; Detroit: Wayne State University Press, 1989), 289.

52. Strauss, "Progress or Return," 273.

53. Beryl Smalley, *The Study of the Bible in the Middle Ages* (1964; Notre Dame: Univ. of Notre Dame Press, 1978), 23.

of history where Augustine made his major contribution. He provided not only the paradigm but the inspiration that would stimulate further speculation. All theories of history, however categorized, beginning with Orosius, bear to some extent the imprint of Augustine's thought. It inspired the theologians of the Middle Ages. While muted to some extent in the Renaissance, it returned in the modern age in a rather disfigured form. Bossuet is a faithful, albeit pedestrian, disciple, and Augustine's shadow hovers over Vico.

The Cartesian version of Augustine influenced a goodly number of thinkers: Comte, even Hegel and Marx were not left untouched. The French Traditionalists and Donoso Cortés followed his wake while appropriating the more sombre aspects of his thought. The majestic proportions of the *Civitas Dei* were greatly reduced, the result of a lengthy process of enfeeblement by which Augustine's thought became a mere simulacrum of itself. Nevertheless, even in a contemporary world that has strayed far from Augustine's convictions, his thought still pulsates in many minds, albeit often subliminally.

CHAPTER 3

Joachim of Fiore

C hristopher Columbus was a man with a mission, a mission reflected
in the signature he often used after 1501, *Xpo ferens* (Christ bearer).
His mission was in great part based on the writings of a Calabrian Abbot,
Joachim of Fiore, who lived about three hundred years previously. Columbus believed that he was inaugurating a new era of Christian expansion and renewal under the auspices of the Spanish crown. His *Libro de
las profecías* (Book of Prophecies), basically a collection of texts, provided
the justification, the apologia, of his program, which he presented to the
Catholic sovereigns Ferdinand and Isabella.[1] With the discovery of new
lands and peoples Columbus surmised that the End Times were approaching, a belief that was confirmed when, during his third voyage, he
convinced himself that he had found the terrestrial paradise, the eschatological goal.

According to Columbus's calculations, one hundred fifty years remained before the end.[2] During this period the gospel would be preached
throughout the world, and Spain would conquer Jerusalem and rebuild

---

1. Christopher Columbus, *Libro de las Profecías,* translation and commentary by
Delno C. West and August Kling (Gainesville: Univ. of Florida Press, 1992). "Notebook of
authorities, statements, opinion and prophecies on the subject of God's holy city and
mountain of Zion, and on the discovery and evangelization of the islands of the Indies
and of all other peoples and nations," is its full title (2).

2. Columbus, *Libro de las Profecías,* 108-9.

the Temple. Hillgarth has pointed out that since the 1470s the expectation of a Messiah burgeoned in the Spanish kingdoms. In 1486, the Marqués de Cádiz circulated an anonymous prophecy that Ferdinand would conquer not only Granada, "but all Africa as far as Ethiopia, Jerusalem, Rome, the Turks, and, in short, the world."[3] A chorus of writers prophesied the day when the King of Spain would possess universal monarchy.[4] Columbus was not limited to the Spanish milieu.

The *Libro de las profecías* accords Joachim a prominent role, only bested by Scripture and the Fathers. He is not only cited seven times — often by way of Joachite literature — but a section of ten folios (67v-77r) headed by ABBAS IOCHIM in large letters is simply missing. These missing folios correspond to part three: "Prophecies of the Future," sandwiched between a pseudo-Joachim quote stating that the age of renewal will come out of Spain and a section on the discovery of scriptural islands and unknown lands.[5] Scholars believe the deletion was purposeful, either by the Inquisition, for fear of its censure, or by friends and relatives attempting to remove Columbus's connection with a suspect doctrine.

Columbus, who on his deathbed donned the habit of a third order Franciscan, had been exposed to Joachite-Franciscan literature, and reflected many of their beliefs. He had great reverence for the Trinity and the Person of the Holy Spirit, was in expectation of a coming "new age," and felt assured that he had received the gift of "spiritual intelligence" for the interpretation of Scripture. In honor of the Trinity, the *Libro de las profecías* is divided into three sections emulating, perhaps consciously, the Abbot Joachim's division of history into three *status* or ages corresponding to the Persons of the Trinity. He was probably influenced by many sources, many rivulets, proceeding from the same principal source — Abbot Joachim of Fiore.

Joachim (1135-1202) was born and died in Calabria on the toe of the Italian boot, an isolated, inhospitable place more appropriate to the life of a desert Father than to a philosopher of history. Pilgrim, priest, monk,

3. J. N. Hillgarth, *The Spanish Kingdoms 1250-1516* (Oxford: Clarendon, 1978), 2:363, 371.

4. Hillgarth, *Spanish Kingdoms,* 364.

5. Columbus, *Libro de las Profecías,* 99.

visionary, artist, scholar, and prophet, Joachim — together with Hildegard of Bingen — was one of the few thinkers whose speculations moved in tandem with their revelations. This provided him with a superb didactic instrument, the *figurae* or images, for their propagation. His first revelation, at the age of thirty-eight, dealt with the mystery of the Trinity. Under its influence he wrote the first book of his *Psalterium decem chordarum* (Psalter of Ten Chords).[6] The title mirrored the *figurae* or image, which appeared to him:[7]

> The shape of a ten-stringed psaltery appeared in my mind. The mystery of the Holy Spirit shone so brightly and clearly . . . that I was . . . impelled to cry out: "What God is as great as our God."

It was his interpretation of history, together with its often-outrageous implications, which guaranteed the survival of his name and thought, notwithstanding the attention his contemporaries gave to his speculations on the Trinity and Antichrist. Although Rupert of Deutz and Anselm of Havelberg had already interpreted history as the progressive revelation of the Trinity, for Joachim, as Marjorie Reeves indicates, "the Trinity was built into the fabric of the time-process in such a way that its very inner relations were expressed therein."[8]

Joachim went against the Augustinian current to the point that Eric Voegelin has called him the great anti-Augustinian in the development of historical speculation.[9] This opinion, only in part justified, is based on Joachim's trinitarian tilt and his florid interpretation of Revelation, a work he believed embraced the fullness of history. History is divided into three *status* or ages. The first, that of the Father, begins with Adam, bears fruit with Abraham, and is consummated in Christ. The second, of the

6. Bernard McGinn, *The Calabrian Abbot: Joachim of Fiore in the History of Western Thought* (New York: Macmillan, 1985), 20.

7. Cited in McGinn, *Calabrian Abbot,* 22.

8. Marjorie Reeves, *Joachim of Fiore and the Prophetic Future* (New York: Harper & Row, 1977), 5-6.

9. Eric Voegelin, *The New Science of Politics* (Chicago: Univ. of Chicago Press, 1952), 111-13.

Son, begins with Ozias, bears fruit with Zachary — the father of John the Baptist — and reaches its consummation in "these times," *viz.,* the final decade of the twelfth century. The third *status,* that of the Holy Spirit, begins with St. Benedict, bears fruit in the succeeding twenty-second generation, and is consummated at the end of the world.[10]

History spirals upwards towards an End Time, which is prefaced by an intra-historical period of peace and well-being. From a human point of view this process aims at a goal: the fullness of Christian liberty. It progresses through the three *status,* stages in its ascent. The first stage is characterized by servitude to the law, the second by filial obedience, the third by the fullness of liberty. History is then the appropriation by man of greater and greater freedom, a process that reflects the changing relation between God and man from that of master/servant to that of father/son to that of friendship. Everything corresponds to this triadic structure and its exigencies.

Each *status* corresponds to a given *ordo* or state of life. The Age of the Father to the "order of the married," that of the Son to the "order of the clergy," and that of the Holy Spirit to the "order of the monks." Each age is characterized by the dominating order, that which sets the tone, as it were, for the whole of society. It is, as stated, an upward ascent with a surprise or two on the way. *Scientia* (knowledge) corresponds to the first age, *sapientia* (wisdom) to the second, and the *'plenitude intellectus'* to the third, the gift that provides a superior insight into Scripture by probing within the letter to unveil the Spirit. This charism proceeds from both testaments in a manner analogous to that by which the Spirit proceeds from both the Father and the Son. The Age of the Father is represented by the twelve patriarchs, that of the Son by the twelve apostles, and that of the Holy Spirit by twelve spiritual men.[11]

The three ages also provide the key to understanding the often-hostile relationship between the Jewish people and Gentiles. Joachim indicates that the Jews flourished in the first age, Gentiles in the second, and both will flourish in the third, the Age of the Holy Spirit. The time for forgive-

10. *Expos.* F. 37 *va.*
11. Reeves, *Prophetic Future,* 14f.

ness, consolation, and conversion is arriving. In the *Tractatus* he indicates that both the Greeks — the Orthodox, who Latin Christians believed were in schism — and the Jews would enter the church at the end of the second *status*.[12] The third *status* would witness a metamorphosis, a new age, a quasi-utopia.

This ascending movement in history, culminating in the third *status*, can be gathered from Scripture, if read with that spiritual insight that Joachim called *"Spiritum intelligentiae,"*[13] given only to those who discipline themselves through prayer, meditation, and study. The third age is privileged. It entails a global renovation that begins in the church and flows out of the church, an age in which the Spirit would act freely, society would be at peace, and the contemplative character would set a tone to be shared proportionately by all orders. It will be an age of monks, but monks superior to those of his day, with whom he grew disenchanted. This order will be the culmination of an ascending spiral, which had its inception with St. Benedict. Joachim distinguished between two new orders whose task lies in the second *status* and the order of contemplatives which pertains to the third *status*, about which he provides no specific details.[14]

The third *status* is truly unique and climactic. It is the "Great Sabbath."[15] The mission of the Holy Spirit, which commenced at Pentecost, will be expanded and enriched. Though some later critics affirmed that Joachim had compromised the role of Christ in salvation history, he stated that the Holy Spirit does not replace Christ but comes to continue the work begun by Christ. In the spiritual men of the third age, "Christ will reign more powerfully."[16] The church itself will not be radically changed or destroyed, as some Joachites believed, but will perdure until

12. McGinn, *Calabrian Abbot,* 35, 46n.122.

13. Marjorie Reeves, *The Influence of Prophecy in the Late Middle Ages* (Oxford: Clarendon, 1969), 13. McGinn cited the *Cronicon Anglicorum* of Ralph of Coggeshill to the effect that Joachim stated that God had given him the "gift of understanding" so that "in God's spirit I very clearly understand all the mysteries of Holy Scripture." *Calabrian Abbot,* 44n.102.

14. Reeves, *Influence,* 137.

15. *Expos.* F. 209 *vb.*

16. *Conc.* V. 67 (F. 96*rb*).

the End, albeit transformed from an *ecclesia activa* to an *ecclesia con-templativa*.[17]

The third age, as Reeves has indicated, "though profoundly spiritual, is both a new age of history and a new kind of society within history."[18] History is basically the account of the progressive spiritualization of mankind that ultimately leads to an intra-historical quasi-utopia. The spiritualized church does not replace the ancient church but raises it to a higher level. This, in practice, heightened disenchantment with the existing church insofar as it was perceived to be moving away from the ideal of the *ecclesia spiritualis*. These contradictions would later be put to use by self-proclaimed disciples who would take Joachim's premises to their ultimate revolutionary conclusions.

In focusing on Scripture as the source of knowledge Joachim, in effect, replaced nature with history as the privileged *locus* of Divine Revelation. In his interpretation of Revelation, the open book carried by the angel descending from heaven symbolizes the revelation of what heretofore had been hidden in the Scriptures. The progressive insight into, and appropriation of, Scripture acts as the index by which to ascertain the movement of history towards its goal. The "letter" of Scripture becomes increasingly more diaphanous, its meaning, its reality, clearer. The momentum increases in the third age with the gift of "spiritual understanding." Joachim's favorite interpretive tool was Revelation (The Apocalypse), which he considered "the key of things past, the knowledge of things to come, the opening of what is sealed, the uncovering of what is hidden."[19]

The Trinity was Joachim's leitmotiv. His principal works can be classified accordingly. The *Liber concordiae* corresponds to the Father: the essential framework of his thought regarding the meaning of history is presented. The *Expositio in Apocalypsum* is mainly concerned with interpretation of the New Testament era, and the *Psalterium decem chordarum* focuses on the *'spiritualis intellectualis'*.[20] His speculations on the Trinity

17. Reeves, *Prophetic Future*, 7.
18. Reeves, "The Originality and Influence of Joachim of Fiore," *Traditio* 36 (1980): 288, 292-93.
19. Cited by McGinn, *Calabrian Abbot*, 146.
20. Reeves, *Influence*, 19, 25.

led to an acerbic polemic with Peter Lombard which, after several turns of fortune, including the possible condemnation of the *Sententiae,* led to Joachim's condemnation by the Fourth Lateran Council.

Perhaps Joachim's most interesting innovation was his use of *figurae* or images, often the point of departure for his most profound speculations. These *figurae* were first perceived in bare outline and later completed in accordance with the ideas that they, together with his prayer, meditation, and associations elicited. We do know that those *figurae* illustrating his main works were later embellished under his direction, and were presented together in the *Liber Figurarum,* which has been described as "a kind of pictorial supplement to his works."[21] Sixteen basic images are here depicted of which possibly the most familiar to scholars is the three intertwined circles representing the Trinity in history adopted from Pedro Alfonso, a Jewish convert with Kabbalistic inclinations.

Another *figurae* worthy of note is that of the threefold tree which embodies the whole of history. These trees expressed in biological terms the unfolding of God's purposes through time. They would be subjected to several variations. When Ubertino de Casale searched for a symbol for the inner growth of history he found it in the image of the tree of history so dear to Joachim.[22] The tree image reached its apotheosis, albeit not historically centered, in the work of Ramon Llull.

Joachim of Fiore died in 1202. At the time it did not seem probable that he had provided the groundwork for one of the most explosive ideologies — if it can be called an ideology — in the course of European history. Yet from Joachim's speculations a storm arose which would ravage Europe and have important consequences in many areas, some of which are still with us today. This storm can be said to have originated in the Joachites, those later disciples who would pass his thought through the filter of their own misconceptions and misinterpretations.

The point of departure for the flight from Joachim's canon and the beginning of a truly revolutionary doctrine is the *Introductorius in Evangelium Aeternum* by Gerardo de Borgo San Donnino (1254). It was, reportedly, an

---

21. McGinn, *Calabrian Abbot,* 107-8.
22. Reeves, *Prophetic Future,* 33.

edition of Joachim's three major works with introduction and glosses,[23] the outgrowth of the enforced sojourn of a Prior of the Florensians carrying Abbot Joachim's principal works at a Franciscan monastery in Pisa. One may conjecture that for Gerardo these works expressed views that had been percolating both in his mind and in the bosom of the Franciscan order. In Reeves's words, Gerardo's book "dropped like a stone into the pool of Paris University in 1255, creating a series of ever-widening ripples."[24]

Gerardo contended that with the coming of the third *status*, expected in 1260, the Old and New Testaments were abrogated and all authority had passed to the *'Evangelium Eternum'*, the Eternal Gospel of the Holy Spirit, given in the works of Joachim entrusted to the Franciscan order.[25] These views were enthusiastically accepted by the rigorist wing of the Franciscans, the *Zelanti* or Spirituals, who later split into several groups of *Fratricelli*. They believed that the original charism of St. Francis had been jeopardized by serious modifications in their rule effected during the Minister-Generalship of Friar Elias. Their views were recorded, somewhat partially, by Salimbene in his *Historia septem tribulationum Ordinis Minorum* (History of the Seven Tribulations of the Order of Minors), an acid indictment of the Conventuals and their leader, Bonaventure.[26]

Strange to say, Bonaventure, who initiated the proceedings against John of Parma, a 'great Joachite' who preceded him as head of the order, sympathized with Joachim's thought to the extent of identifying the angel of the Apocalypse (7:2) with St. Francis and elaborating a theology of history in his *Collationes*.[27] For his part, Thomas Aquinas took a dim view of Joachim's speculations. He overtly condemned *"ipsa doctrina Ioachimi"*[28] and in the *Summa Theologiae* discusses the question whether the "new law" will perdure until the end of the world, the third objection nicely reproduc-

---

23. The completed mss. has not survived.

24. Reeves, *Influence*, 187f.

25. Reeves, *Prophetic Future*, 33.

26. *Obras de San Buenaventura* (edicion bilique) edited by L. Amoros, B. Aperribay y M. Oromi (Madrid: BAC, 1955), 1:19-20.

27. Refer to J. Ratzinger, *The Theology of History in St. Bonaventure* (Chicago: Franciscan Herald Press, 1971).

28. Aquinas *Op. Theol.* ii, 105 (68).

ing Joachim's three *status* theory. Thomas maintains that the promise of the Spirit was fulfilled at Pentecost, that there is no reason to expect a "new law" of the Holy Spirit, and insists that to affirm that the gospel of Christ is not the gospel of the Kingdom is extremely foolish *(stultissimum)*.[29]

The Spirituals, after the trial of John of Parma, continued a largely underground existence with strongholds in Provence, Tuscany, and the Marches led by men such as Peter Olivi and Angel Clareno, the historian. It was Fra Dolcino and his Apostolic Brethren who moved from revolutionary preaching to revolution in practice, trusting that a new outpouring of the Holy Spirit would generate a political golden age. The "great whore" of the existing church would be overthrown by violence as a propedeutic to the coming utopia. Dolcino took to arms and was defeated and executed.[30]

There were many other outbursts of Joachitism. Among those was Cola de Rienzo, a utopian revolutionary who proclaimed a new Roman Republic and named himself Tribune, a friend of the *Fratricelli,* who was slaughtered by the Roman mob in October 1354. Perhaps the most bizarre of these offshoots was the earlier Amaurians, whose origins lead back to the Parisian master Amaury of Bene. They divided history into its trinitarian stages — each age distinguished by an appropriate incarnation. The first (Age of the Father) was incarnated in Abraham, the second (Age of the Son) in Christ, the third (Age of the Holy Spirit) in the Amaurians themselves, who would lead all men on the road to becoming "spirtituals."[31] Nor should the cult of Gugliema, furthered by Manfreda and Andreas Saramita, be forgotten. This sect took Joachite principles to their ultimate bizarre conclusion and in so doing adumbrated today's radical feminism. If the utopian upset is to be complete, they urged, the new incarnation of the Godhead must take place in the feminine sex. Consequently, they believed that the Holy Spirit had been incarnated in a woman — Gugliema — that the new Pope would be a woman — Manfreda — and her cardinals would also be . . . women.[32]

---

29. Thomas Aquinas, *Summa Theologiae* 1-2 q. 106 a. 4.

30. Bernard McGinn, *Visions of the End* (New York: Columbia Univ. Press, 1979), 226-27.

31. N. Cohn, *The Pursuit of the Millennium* (Fairlawn: Essential Books, 1957), 159-60.

32. Reeves, "Originality and Influence," 249-50.

The rather tarnished line of descent of the Calabrian Abbot's thought passed through the Franciscan Spirituals and several others who took up or concocted the powerful mythologies of the Last World Emperor and the Angelic Pope. They were to play an important role both in religious and political movements, and even after their demise, left indelible traces in the collective unconscious. When enthusiasm waned and salvation seemed to elude religious and political nostrums, the heirs of these enthusiasts turned to more worldly vehicles of salvation: revolution, science and exploration, art.

In the Renaissance Joachim is present in Tomasso Campanella's *City of the Sun,* a realm of love under a reformed Pope. Botticelli's so-called "eschatological Nativity" has been called by Saxl one of the great documents of Joachimist thought . . . carried to a high point of ecstasy.[33] The Abbot himself was portrayed as an artist. According to one legend he appeared in Venice to direct the portrayal of SS. Francis and Dominic on the mosaics of St. Marks.[34] It is evident that what Yeats in "The Tables of the Law" called "that hidden substance of God which is color and music and softness and a sweet odor,"[35] exercised its potent charm even after his death, and passed over into Protestantism in the revolutionary utopianism of Thomas Munzer, who led a peasant uprising crushed at the battle of Frankenhausen (1525).

The Joachimist influence reached Columbus from several sources, among which Peter John Olivi's *Postilla super apocalypsum* can probably be counted. Perhaps closer at hand is Ubertino de Casale's *Arbor Vitae crucifixae Iesu,* which was translated into Spanish for Queen Isabella, and the works of Arnold of Villanova, physician to the Court of Aragon. Perhaps also Francisco Examemis, who followed Joachimist chronological patterns and predicted the advent of a *princeps mundi* who would appear at the twilight of the second *status*.[36] The vision Columbus culled from these sources helped to provide the impetus for his remarkable career as admiral of the ocean seas.

33. F. Saxl, *Journal of the Warburg and Courtauld Institutes,* (1942), 5:84f.
34. Reeves, *Prophetic Future,* 97.
35. Reeves, *Prophetic Future,* 171.
36. Columbus, *Libro de las Profecías,* 32ff.

Joachim's influence even reached the modern age. Lessing's *Educa-tion of the Human Race* restates the theme of the reign of love on earth while presenting the "gospel" of the coming golden age. This would be-come a mainstay of Saint-Simonism and pass on to Comte, Saint-Simon's secretary, who viewed Joachim as one of his predecessors.[37] Lowith, in an interesting appendix to his *Meaning in History,* indicates that the most original attempt to establish the reign of the Spirit philo-sophically was that of Schelling. Schelling appealed to a triadic structure of history with a different tilt. The first age is that of Peter, the apostle of the Father, which corresponds to Roman Catholicism. The second is that of Paul, apostle of the Son, corresponding to Protestantism. The third, that of John, apostle of the Spirit, will lead humanity to the fullness of truth . . . the perfect religion of mankind.[38]

In these schemes, to which could be added those of Fichte, Hegel, Novalis, and even Marx, the Joachimist inspiration is excised of its reli-gious sediment and the church relegated to the outer darkness. What is retained in spite of the ongoing process of secularization is an optimistic view of historical movement, an interpretation of the inner workings of this movement, and the zealotry of its sectaries — from *Fratricelli* to Marxists — firm in the belief that they are marching on the path deter-mined by history. As Josef Pieper has observed, "the history of a 'New Heaven' and a 'New Earth' in its secularized and degenerate shape has become and remains a historical agent of the utmost significance."[39] It has certainly become a perennial lure, a temptation. Ernst Bloch, in the mid-twentieth century, declared: "Above Christian and Jew: messianism and the *Tertium Testamentum.*"[40]

---

37. Frank E. Manuel, *Shapes of Philosophical History* (Stanford: Stanford Univ. Press, 1965), 43f.

38. Karl Lowith, *Meaning in History* (Chicago: Univ. of Chicago Press, 1949), 209-10.

39. Josef Pieper, *The End of Time: A Meditation on the Philosophy of History,* trans. Michael Bullock (New York: Pantheon, 1954), 68.

40. Cited by J. Moltmann in his introduction to Ernst Bloch's *Man on His Own,* trans. E. B. Ashton (1959; New York: Herder & Herder, 1970), 20.

CHAPTER 4

Augustinian Variations

I

Franz Rosenzweig observed that the Scriptures constituted the first conversation of mankind, a conversation in which gaps of half and whole millennia occur between speech and response.[1] St. Paul attempted to find the answer to the question of the third chapter of Genesis — the expulsion from Eden — by questioning the words of the twentieth chapter of Exodus — the giving of the Decalogue. Augustine replied with the *Civitas Dei.* Bishop Otto of Freising (1111-1158) replied with his *Chronicon sive Historia de duabus civitatibus.*[2] Later still, Donoso Cortés would reply with the *Ensayo sobre el catolicismo, el liberalismo y el socialismo.* Conversation at a distance between personalities of unequal genius and disparate temperament is bound to be as illuminating as it is frustrating.

A study of Bishop Otto's *Two Cities* shows that Augustine's majestic conception has suffered a sea change. Augustine wrote an *apologia* for a surging Christianity against the remnants of a declining civilization, truly alive only in libraries. Otto attempted to come to terms with a civilization

1. Franz Rosenzweig, "On the Scriptures," in *Franz Rosenzweig: His Life and Thought,* ed. Nahum N. Glatzer (New York: Schocken, 1974), 260.
2. Otto of Freising, *The Two Cities,* trans. C. C. Mierow, ed. A. P. Evans and C. Knapp (New York: Columbia Univ. Press, 1928).

as yet unfixed, slowly emerging from the slough of a lengthy period of turbulence. The weighty principles of the *Civitas Dei* are contracted, their substance weakened. The Two Cities are flattened if not merged. The City of God is identified with the Church aspiring, reaching out, to its completion in the unchangeable City of the other world.

Albeit pervasive, Augustine's influence is muted. Apart from the Bible (Jerome's translation) and that of Cicero, Aristotle, and the poets (Vergil, Horace, and Ovid), Otto's major influence was probably Paulus Orosius's *Seven Books,* itself based on Bishop Eusebius's *Ecclesiastical History.* The *Two Cities* covers the period from creation to 1146 in seven books with the eighth book dealing with the End Times and the World to Come. The book was continued by another Otto, a monk of St. Blaise, who took the history up to the year 1209.[3]

The bishop's historical speculations are centered on the succession of world empires. Following St. Jerome's commentary on the book of Daniel that names four empires, the Assyrian-Babylonian, the Medo-Persian, the Macedonian, and the Roman, he emulates Orosius in substituting Carthage for the Medo-Persian. Moreover, he follows the Roman Empire, destined to last until the end of the world, through its Byzantine, Frankish, and German metamorphoses. In a letter to Rainald he states:[4]

> I shall briefly explain the order in which this history proceeds . . .
> that there were from the beginning of the world four principal king-
> doms which stood out above the rest, and they are to endure to the
> world's end, succeeding one another in accordance with the laws of
> the universe. . . . I have therefore set down the rulers of these king-
> doms listed in chronological sequence . . . and I have recorded their
> names down to the present emperor, speaking of the other king-
> doms only incidentally to make manifest the fluctuation of events.

Otto was a spiritual realist, a trait perhaps inherited from the Cistercian Order to which he belonged. Transitoriness and decay characterize the

---

3. Otto of Freising, *Two Cities,* Intro., 45.

4. Cited in Otto of Freising, *Two Cities,* Intro., 29-30.

mutable world; an element of *Weltschmerz* marks his character and is present in his work. The history was written "in bitterness of spirit led thereto by the turbulence of that unsettled time which preceded grace. . . . I wove together, in the manner of a tragedy, their sodden aspects."[5] In the prologue to the *Gesta Friderici I Imperatoris* he distinguishes between "the plain speech of history" — the account of historical events without commentary — and "the loftier pinnacles of philosophy" to which he doubtless aspired.[6] In spite of his rather simplistic notion of the goal of the historical genre — "to extol the famous deeds of violent men in order to invite the hearts of mankind to virtue . . . [and] veil in silence the dark doings of the base,"[7] Bishop Otto succeeded in touching the outskirts of the philosophy of history.

Otto had a high opinion of philosophy, perhaps due to years spent studying at the Parisian schools. Philosophy together with law he considered forerunners of the Messiah as they have provided men with the capacity of understanding the higher reaches of the human spirit. He adopted several of the misconceptions of his age: notably that Jeremiah was the teacher of Plato, who was cognizant of all Christian truth excepting only the Incarnation. Greatly intellectualized, the bishop affirms that the scholastic method outweighs any human authority.[8] However, his criticism of Abelard and Arnold of Brescia[9] indicates that his intellectualism was not unbounded.

His tilt to the tragic was to some extent muted by his belief in the sovereign lordship of the Divine Will and concern over the approach of the End Times. The *'translatio'* (transference) of empire from the Romans to the Greeks, the Greeks to the Franks, and finally, the Franks to the Germans, moves in this direction. A strong and robust people inherit the sovereignty from a people grown weak and senile. Otto follows Hugo of St.

5. Otto of Freising, *Two Cities,* 89.
6. Cited in Otto of Freising, *Two Cities,* Intro., 51-52.
7. Otto of Freising, *Two Cities,* Intro., 25.
8. Otto of Freising, *Two Cities,* VIII, 9; IV, 18.
9. Otto of Freising, *The Deeds of Frederick Barbarossa,* trans. C. C. Mierow (New York: Columbia Univ. Press, 1953), I, 48 (pp. 84-87).

Victor who, in his *De vanitate mundi,* adumbrating Hegel, taught that the world progresses from East to West:[10]

> All human power or learning had its origin in the East but is coming to an end in the West that thereby the transitoriness and decay of all things human may be displayed.

His interest in history — history for its own sake — is greater than that of Augustine, for whom it is no more than a signpost pointing to greater realities. Otto's attempt to fill in the historical gaps often borders on the tedious. Although the Cities can be traced back to the creation of man, Bishop Otto endeavors to proceed "in such a way that we shall not lose the thread of history" following the gradual rise of primitive man to civilization.[11] The Roman Empire — destined to perdure until the end — marks the center of his speculations. In the wake of Orosius and Eusebius he stresses its role as protector of the Christian church. Augustine's vision of the Two Cities falls victim to the exigencies of *realpolitik* represented by the church and the new Christian empire. The substructure of history is no longer the continuing struggle between the Two Cities but the providential succession of empires preparing the way for the church-empire leading to the last days. Though hardly enthusiastic, the Imperial Bishop believed that the church was destined to grow into an earthly kingdom, that its burgeoning would be accompanied by the progressive decline of the Roman Empire.[12] The last empire, the ultimate manifestation of the Roman, will be utterly destroyed by "that stone hewn from a mountain, not by human hands" (Daniel 2:34), which is the church. For Otto the City of God is localized in the church in the wake of the Incarnation:[13]

> I seem . . . to have composed a history not of two cities but virtually of one only, which I call the Church. . . . I must call them properly but one — composite, however, as the grain mixed with chaff.

10. Otto of Freising, *Two Cities,* V Prol. (pp. 322-23).
11. Otto of Freising, *Two Cities,* III Prol. (pp. 217-22).
12. Otto of Freising, *Two Cities,* IV, 4 (pp. 280-83).
13. Cited in Otto of Freising, *Two Cities,* Intro., 67-68.

Rome casts a powerful shadow! Why did Christ, Otto asks, desire to be "enrolled" in the Roman State? The answer: "He had come to fashion his own city in a strange and inexplicable manner from the city of the world.[14] The Church of God displays two roles: the sacerdotal and the royal. It is a great net that encompasses good and evil under the aegis of dual authority. Otto's notion of authority was blatantly imperial. As he wrote to his nephew, Emperor Frederick Barbarossa: "Kings alone . . . set above the laws and reserved to be weighted in the divine balances, are not held in restraint by the laws of the world."[15] The church will inherit this authority.

Historical coincidence and parallel events make for serious reflection. Rome was founded on Palatine hill at about the same time that Isaiah and Hosea prophesied in Palestine. The Incarnation is the point of departure for the spread of the Heavenly City, the Kingdom of Christ, which is the church.[16] However, when the apostles were crowned with martyrdom in Rome, the secular prestige of the City began to decline. Otto lauds Constantine, who was commissioned by God to accomplish the feat of drawing out the Kingdom from the City of the World. He received both faith and love "whereby he might exalt (God's) City with many honors . . . and enrich it with many treasures."[17] The Donation of Constantine seems to act as the beginning of the end for secular Imperial Rome.

Civilization and authority moves from East to West. This *'translatio'* took place when Charlemagne was crowned by the Pope as the sixty-ninth emperor, counting from Augustus Caesar. After being transferred to the Franks it was later passed on to the Germans with Arnaulf, the eighty-fourth emperor. Although the church is destined to be both executioner and replacement of the empire, it nevertheless will pass through the crucible of persecution. Beginning with violent persecutions under pagan kings, the attacks will continue, launched by heretics and hypocrites only to peak at the End when Satan will "pour forth" by means of the Antichrist the strength he has collected throughout history.[18]

14. Otto of Freising, *Two Cities*, VIII Prol. (pp. 453-56).
15. Otto of Freising, *Two Cities*, III, 6 (p. 230).
16. Otto of Freising, *Two Cities*, VII Prol. (p. 404).
17. Otto of Freising, *Two Cities*, IV Prol. (p. 271).
18. Otto of Freising, *Two Cities*, VIII, 2 (p. 457).

The *Gesta,* written at Emperor Frederick Barbarossa's request, and based in part on an outline he furnished, was Bishop Otto's swan song. He died after having written the first two books, the final two written in a less exalted style by the monk Rahewin. It was his last tribute to the Hohenstaufen and its *regnum Teutonicorum.* Not only a great churchman and scholar, he was responsible for the first trace of the dissemination of Aristotle's books in Germany.[19] His efforts at elaborating a philosophy of history encountered in the *Gesta*[20] are dense and convoluted. Nevertheless, his conception of universal history — as dim as it appears compared to the *Civitas Dei* — chained to the fortunes of a Roman Empire undergoing gradual transmutation into the City of God, had no little influence on the succeeding ages.

In spite of his pessimism, Otto never lost his faith in the existence of an ever-active Divine Will determining the course of human events. His ascetic inclination, which encouraged the flight from the *Civitas Mundi* to the *Civitas Dei,* in effect secularized the Cities and centered attention on the church and empire. A subtle appraisal of future possibilities grounded on Scripture gives way to a stark apocalypticism. But he never wavered in his belief that the City of God, the community of the good, would perdure and that it is by means of reason, "the inner man, made after the likeness of the Creator," that man can escape and find release from the things of time.[21]

II

If the Bishop of Freising is an interesting, albeit uninspired, variation of an Augustine subjected to the force of gravity, Hildegard von Bingen (1098-1179) is a definite novelty touching the spectacular, although speculation on history comprises only a modest portion of her multifaceted oeuvre. An interesting eccentric of genius: her thoughts original, her vocabulary innovative, her visions bizarre, her person elusive. She strides from the depths of a *'paupercula'* — poor little woman — to the heights of

---

19. Otto of Freising, *Two Cities, Intro.,* 41.
20. Otto of Freising, *Deeds,* I, 5 (pp. 31-40); I, 55 (pp. 90-94); I, 62 (pp. 104-6).
21. Otto of Freising, *Two Cities,* I Prol. (p. 93); VII Prol. (p. 402).

the voice of the Living Light, a status of which she appears to have taken full advantage. Beginning as a disciple of the anchoress Jutta (†1136) she ended her days as Abbess of the Benedictine convent of Rupertsberg. Writer, reformer, abbess, preacher, counselor, physician, musician, composer, theologian, polemicist against the Cathars, prophet, Hildegard can also, with good reason, be considered the harbinger of feminism, environmentalism, and even the hospital system.

The center of her activity was the visionary life she was gifted with as a child at the age of three and which continued until her death at over eighty years of age. Her biographer states:[22]

> It was in 1141 when God flashed into her life like a mighty fire and an exceedingly bright light. . . . He made her, the seer, into a prophet: "Write what you see and hear."

She had previously informed Jutta and now, because of this watershed vision, spoke to the monk Volmar who encouraged her to record these visions. This she did. The outcome was her first and perhaps most important work, the *Scivias*.[23] It was written in Latin, the medium of high culture, and quite a feat for a woman of admittedly negligible learning. She put "the entire work of creation" into "pictures of magnificent creative power" that reflect and supplement one another.[24] They mirror Hildegard's fascination with the presence of God in the world — with his immanence. The universe receives its life from God, who, by becoming man, consecrated the world.[25] The closeness, the intimacy, between God and the cosmos often verges on pantheism and remains a disturbing element of her thought.

The great light that she experienced as a child so upset her that she saw much that was strange and spoke much that was strange. The light presented itself to her in two forms. First of all, as the *umbra viventis*

---

22. *The Life of the Holy Hildegard by the Monks Gottfried and Theodore,* trans. James McGrath (Collegeville: The Liturgical Press, 1995), 6.

23. Hildegard of Bingen, *Scivias,* trans. Mother Columbia Hart and Jane Bishop (New York: Paulist Press, 1990).

24. *Life,* 6-7.

25. *Life,* 15.

luminis — the shadow of the living light — which always accompanied her; rarer, as extraordinary promptings "like flashing flames and clouds moving in the pure air," immediate apprehension.[26] This divine light vaulted an insignificant anchoress to European prominence in spite of galling physical and psychological maladies. Several of her visions have been analyzed as migraine aura effects.[27]

As did Joachim of Fiore, Hildegard von Bingen claimed that her visionary gifts gave her a privileged insight into the meaning of Scripture, and even the thought of some philosophers.[28] Her extensive correspondence reflects her prominence, style, and changes of mood. When Pope Eugenius III read sections of her work to assembled clergy she received the highest plaudits. Yet, to the same Pope she wrote in 1148:

> Now once again he speaks to you, he who is the living light which illumines the heights and depths and reveals itself even in the innermost areas of the heart of those who listen.[29]

Hildegard was a prolific author. A scientific encyclopedia, the *Physica,* supplemented by *Causae et Curae,* a handbook of diseases and their remedies, followed the *Scivias* (1151). The liturgical poetry and music she composed was arranged in a cycle entitled *Symphonia Armonie Celestium Revelationum,* familiar to contemporary musicologists. The second and third volumes of her visionary trilogy, the *Liber Vitae Meritorum* and the *Liber Divinorum Operum,* were completed in 1163 and 1174. She also wrote several *opuscula,* including an exposition of the Benedictine Rule and the Athanasian Creed as well as an odd work called the *Lingua Ignota* (Unknown Language), a list of some nine hundred artificial nouns with an accompanying German glossary.[30]

26. Sabina Flanagan, *Hildegard of Bingen: A Visionary Life* (1989; London: Routledge, 1998), 9.

27. Charles Singer, *From Magic to Science* (New York: Dover, 1958), 231-32.

28. *Life,* 101.

29. Cited in *Life,* 104.

30. Cf. Barbara Newman, *Sister of Wisdom: St. Hildegard's Theology of the Feminine* (Berkeley: Univ. of California Press, 1987), 10ff.

The "pictures" that so impressed her biographers and contemporaries are superb avenues of approach to her thought. In one, Hildegard is depicted receiving the fire of charity from heaven while transcribing the vision on wax tablets. The nun Richardis assists her while the monk Volmar copies the text into a book. In another, God is envisioned as a winged man whose head and shoulders rise into the pure ether, a gigantic figure, an active fire, who surveys and sustains the cosmos, filling it with boundless vitality.[31] Like Bishop Otto, the abbess had a favorable opinion of philosophy: a further plate contrasts Caritas, a fair and noble lady, to *Amor secularis,* her face black and scarlet, and to a female merchant (philosophy) "who establishes every art and discovers the crystal of faith which leads to God."[32]

A picture that takes us to the core of Hildegard's thoughts on history is the Wheel of Charity, which rests in the center of the wheel of eternity and history. It is divided into quadrants. The upper left portion is green, representing the eternal freshness of the world in the mind of God prior to creation. The upper right is red, indicating the glory of the redeemed universe. The bottom half is a mingling of pallor and darkness, denoting the anguish of time. This is the province of history. The circumference of the wheel represents the Fatherhood of God, its center the motherhood of Mary.[33]

Pallor and darkness between green and red, history — the life of man — is set between the eternal freshness of the Divine Mind and the transfigured reality of the redeemed universe. *Viriditas* (greenness) is the key symbol, the principle of life, which flows from the life-creating power of God. In Peter Drucke's words, it is "the greenness of a paradise which knows no fall."[34] In her poem to St. Disibod she refers to him as the *"veriditas digiti Dei,"* the 'greenness' of the finger of God.[35]

This is anchored to her Eastern-influenced conception of the Fall.

31. Newman, *Sister of Wisdom,* 18.
32. Cited by Newman, *Sister of Wisdom,* 84.
33. Hildegard, *De Operatione Dei,* III, 10. Lucca Biblioteca Statale, Codex lat. 1942.
34. Peter Drucke, "Tradition and Innovation in Medieval Western Color Imagery," *Eranos Jahrbuch* III (1972): 82, 84.
35. Flanagan, *Hildegard,* 90. *The Wisdom of Hildegard,* ed. Fiona Bowie (Grand Rapids: Eerdmans, 1977), 44.

Through human prevarication the entire universe and all it contains suffered grievous injury. The elements were in harmony prior to the Fall, but after this were disturbed and remain in a state of mingled confusion (*'mistio'*). Hildegard urges that God desires a "clean earth" and will not allow it to be harmed or destroyed through human actions. At the end, subjected to the "melting pot" of the Last Judgment, the elements will take on a new, eternal harmony corresponding to the New Heaven.[36]

The present world, though fallen, retains traces of *viriditas,* as well as velleities towards a higher realm of existence. The human voice aspires to the original beauty of Adam's voice; precious gems retain some of their original brilliance reflected in their curative powers. Holiness generates *viriditas.* The abbess restores the cosmos/microcosmos relationship destroyed by Augustine. However, she does not resuscitate pagan naturalism. Instead, she takes the lead from Christian belief by relating the prologue of the Gospel of St. John to the first chapter of Genesis.[37] Though the cosmos/microcosmos relation can be traced back through Bernardus Silvestres to Plato's *Timaeus,* the Incarnation is here the center that establishes the link between the constitution of the cosmos, the qualities of the soul, and the structure of the body.

The feminine is of great importance. Hildegard's "feminism" was primarily grounded on those scriptural passages that were interpreted by twelfth-century exegetes as portraying *Sophia, Sapientia,* Wisdom, as God's feminine consort and collaborator in the work of creation: Proverbs 8, Ecclesiasticus 24, and the Wisdom of Solomon 7–9. *Sapientia* creates the cosmos by existing within it, her ubiquity expressed through the image of circular motion. The feminine seems to reflect God's immanence in her thought, the masculine his transcendence. The abbess exclaims: "O woman, what a splendid being you are! For you set your foundation in the sun, and you have conquered the world."[38]

Hildegard was very much disturbed by the unsettled age in which she

36. Hildegard, *Scivias,* III, 12, 4-15, pp. 516-20.
37. Flanagan, *Hildegard,* 136ff.; Newman, *Sister of Wisdom,* 20ff.
38. *The Letters of Hildegard of Bingen,* trans. Joseph L. Baird and Rodd K. Ehrman (New York: Oxford Univ. Press, 1994), vol. 1, letter 52r: "To the Congregation of Nuns" (p. 128).

lived. This served as an incentive to historical speculation. The male rulers, religious and secular, had lost their virility and turned to effeminate ways. This *'muliebre tempus'* — womanish age — contrasted strongly to the "paradisiacal age" of virginal nature and the "apostolic age" of masculine strength. In a letter to Abbot Helengerus (c. 1170) she mentions an Age of Milk — before the flood — of Pablum — the time of Noah — of Mastication — the time of Abraham — all of which led to the end of childhood in Moses, who fulfills the previous ages and points to a New Age that begins with the Son of God and is to be gradually revealed to the whole of creation.[39]

The present "womanish age," which commenced about the time of her birth, is castigated unmercifully. Those vain, worldly prelates, who have lost their zeal for the word of God, "possess the virtues of neither sex and the vices of both."[40] This degradation of *Ecclesia* by those who should have made her beautiful will bring untold woes. In a tirade that later would be interpreted as a prophecy of the Protestant Reformation, the abbess sees princes conspiring against prelates, stripping them of their wealth and banishing them. The people will turn against them in the name of God and monasteries will be dissolved at sword point.

The structure of history fascinated her. As Newman suggests, the very figure of *Ecclesia* can be said to personify history, an image that can be read from the top downwards with reference to the successive ages of the world. Moreover, the last five visions of the *Liber Divinorum Operum* introduce the notion of time into the timeless description of the created universe. The figure displays six wings adorned with mirrors bearing inscriptions which represent both the six days of creation and the six ages of the world. Time and eternity constitute a single whole in the form of a wheel with a line projected across its center.[41] *Caritas* presides over the wheel with the various colors on the wheel representing different stages of prehistory moving towards the Incarnation and from the Incarnation to the End Times.

---

39. *Letters*, vol. 1, letter 77r: "To Abbot Helengerus" (pp. 168-71).
40. *Letters*, 242.
41. *Letters*, 246; Flanagan, *Hildegard*, 148.

Perhaps the most substantial text on the subject of history is found in the eleventh vision of the *Scivias*. It is dedicated to the End Times and runs to some eighteen pages. From the "womanish time" to the End, *Ecclesia* will be tried in the crucible of five succeeding ages that Hildegard represents as five beasts: (1) the *fiery dog,* a time of tepidness and misplaced zealousness, of men who do not burn with the justice of God; (2) the *yellow lion,* a period of mindless warmongers ignoring God's righteousness; (3) the *pale horse,* persons trapped in a whirlwind of sin and pleasure to the neglect of virtue; (4) the *black pig,* men who wallow in the mud of impurity and blacken themselves with unnatural sins such as homosexuality; (5) the *grey wolf,* an age of cunning, plunder, spoilage, division, and conquest, which leads to the End Times when "the error of errors will rise from Hell to Heaven."[42]

This last, seventh, age will be catastrophic. The status of Jesus will be questioned. He will be accused of being a madman. The church will be reproached for a multiplicity of vices. Those who should love the church will persecute her unmercifully. But when the heat of the day is vanished and cold burgeons then Christ will manifest himself to the world. The New Jerusalem will descend and the depredations of the Fall will be corrected. Together with all things, the elements will be purified and whatever was foul will disappear as does salt in water. The elements will shine brightly, purged of all blackness and filth.[43]

Though both Hildegard and Bishop Otto occupy branches of the Augustinian tree, they differ markedly both in theory and in personality. The abbess stands halfway between Otto and Joachim of Fiore, following the latter more in style than in content. For her, history in the wake of the Incarnation is interrupted by a sharp decline through six ages until the End Times, the Antichrist, and the final *renovatio*. There is no interruption, as in Joachim, in the downward course of history, no intrahistorical age of the Holy Spirit. Both Hildegard and Joachim were visionaries. In a way, Hildegard prepares the way for a drastic departure from the Augustinian path in the person of Joachim of Fiore.

---

42. Hildegard, *Scivias,* III, I-III, 5, pp. 494-95.
43. Hildegard, III, 12, 4-15, pp. 516-20.

Hildegard was not without future influence. In 1220, Gabino of Eberbad, a Cistercian prior, compiled an anthology of her prophecies and apocalyptic writings . . . the *Pentachronon*. It survives in over a hundred manuscripts. In the Renaissance, Johannes Trithemius (1462-1516) who passed this interest on to his pupil, Paracelsus, lauded her. Jacques Lefèvre d'Étaples, the author of a work on natural magic, published the first edition of the *Scivias* in 1513. Centuries later her notion of the feminine divine would resurface in the works of Vladimir Soloviev (†1900) and Maura Boeckeler.[44] Today, Hildegard is in danger of becoming a New Age guru, as witnessed by the splurge of publications dedicated to the more esoteric aspects of her thought.

44. Newman, *Sister of Wisdom,* 259-65.

CHAPTER 5

The Renaissance Interlude

The Renaissance was an exotic parenthesis in European history, a hermetic interlude, a display and explosion that served as bridge from the Middle Ages to modernity. A passive return to the paradigms of the ancient world, often arbitrarily interpreted, occurred, promoting a spectacular burgeoning of the plastic arts and literature. Its genius resided in the interpretation of the present through the optics of a highly chromatic past. This involved a return to the cyclic conception of time and led to a muting of historical speculation. Ancient texts, such as those of Aristotle and Polybius, popularized the cyclical view, as did those hermetic texts supposedly of great antiquity (actually from the second and third centuries AD) that mesmerized the age and exercised a strong influence on its thinkers and artists.

The prominence of this alien intruder in the Renaissance led to a widely felt sympathy for the radical and heterodox. Certain heterodox currents of medieval thought were taken up and exacerbated. Petrarch (1304-1374) was one of the first to sound the alarm, chiding those "new theologians," who, unsparing of the Doctors of the Church, "soon will not respect the Apostles . . . nor the Gospel, and eventually will let loose their frivolous talk against Christ himself."[1] Whatever the depredations of

1. Letter to Boccaccio, Aug. 28, 1364, cited in *The Renaissance Philosophy of Man,* ed. Ernst Cassirer, Paul Oskar Kristeller, and John Herman Randall Jr. (Chicago: Univ. of Chicago Press, 1948), 140.

these thinkers, and the obscuring of historical speculation is certainly one, there is one product of the Renaissance that is of substantial importance for the later revival of the philosophy of history: the utopia.

Mumford is somewhat off course when he maintains that the classic utopias beginning with Plato had little influence; no direct role can be attributed to them in the genesis of great social changes. Utopias stultify, for once perfection is achieved, stasis sets in.[2] However, it can be argued that utopias, as they are creations of the mind, cannot be actualized in the concrete world. Perfection is never attained. Utopias remain on the horizon, impossible dreams. Like the sirens, utopias lure humanity to ever greater efforts that are doomed to failure, yet, as principles of action, lie at the ground of political and social upheaval. In this way, they have an important role in the unfolding of history and must be taken into account. The very term "utopia" was coined in the Renaissance, which set the stage for later developments of substantial importance.

However, this is hardly the aspect of the Renaissance that has fascinated scholars, artists, and the cultivated public. The most spectacular flowering took place in the plastic arts and in literature. Humanism was probably the most pervasive element within Renaissance culture.[3] It tilted thinking to the secular, stressed study of the Greek and Latin classics, and dismissed logic. It succeeded in making the Latin authors more widely known and translated a great number of Greek texts into Latin. Logic was excluded from the traditional *Trivium* (grammar, rhetoric, and logic); history, moral and Greek philosophy were added. Poetry was enthroned as its most important member.[4]

In the arts a steady progression is encountered from its origin with Cimabue and Giotto to its acme in the sixteenth century. This corresponded to that ever more intense craving for beauty that so impressed the young Nietzsche. The "arts" — the beaux arts — were separated from the "crafts," the descendents of the Greek *techne*. This was based on

2. Lewis Mumford, *The Pentagon of Power: The Myth of the Machine* (New York: Harcourt Brace Jovanovich, 1973), 2:209-11.

3. *Renaissance Philosophy of Man,* 5.

4. Paul Oskar Kristeller, *Studies in Renaissance Thought and Letters* (Rome: Edizioni di Storia e Letteratura, 1993), 3:568.

Vasari's *Arti del Designo* and took place institutionally in Florence about the year 1563 when the painters, sculptors, and architects ended their connection with the craftsmen's guilds and formed the *Accademia del Designo,* which became the prototype of all later institutions.[5] The arts preserved an important pragmatic aspect, as illustrated by Leonardo's post as "chief engineer" to the army of Cesare Borgia.

A superb summary of the principal characteristics of the age is provided by the four chapter headings in Burckhardt's *The Civilization of the Renaissance in Italy:* "The State as a Work of Art"; "The Development of the Individual"; "The Revival of Antiquity"; and "The Discovery of the World and Man."[6] Within the complex and often frightening web of passion and politics that was the Renaissance, a new world was forming. The depredations of the *Condottieri* and the horrors of internecine bloodshed only increased the lure of a resuscitated Rome. Venice became the center of political science. Florence enjoyed "the most elevated political thought and the most varied forms of human development."[7] Machiavelli viewed his city as a living organism and, in his *Arte della Guerra,* approached the border of the philosophy of history by recognizing a law of continuous though not uniform development in republican institutions.[8]

The cult of the individual, often exaggerated, was taken to new heights. The "mirrors" of the Middle Ages, which attempted to mould the person in accordance with a given model, the ultimate paradigm being Christ, were shattered in an orgy of self-affirmation. The multifaceted man — *L'uomo universale* — became the goal of human life, the passion for fame its motive force, in an age characterized by Burckhardt as one of overstrained and despairing passions.[9] The atmosphere of wholesale extravagance gave added impetus to the revival of antiquity in which books often took precedence over artifacts and were accepted as the basis of all knowledge. Humanities controlled the writing of history which, in this

5. Kristeller, *Studies in Renaissance Thought,* 3:557, 572.

6. Jacob Burckhardt, *The Civilization of the Renaissance in Italy,* trans. by S. G. C. Middlemore (London: Penguin, 1990).

7. Burckhardt, *Civilization of the Renaissance,* 63, 66.

8. Burckhardt, *Civilization of the Renaissance,* 160.

9. Burckhardt, *Civilization of the Renaissance,* 72.

epoch, inclined towards either a servile imitation of the ancients or towards the colorful and bizarre in an effort to excite, charm, or overwhelm the reader.[10]

The first step towards the Renaissance exaltation of man was taken by Manetti, who, in his *De dignitate et excellentia homini,* gave a tardy reply to Pope Innocent III's treatise on the woeful state of mankind.[11] Marsilio Ficino's *Platonic Theology* contains several passages that emphasize the excellence and dignity of man, marking his centrality and universality. The theme reaches its apotheosis in Pico della Mirandola's *Oration on the Dignity of Man,* where it became persistent, systematic, and exclusive, exceeding by far the modest encomiums found in Greek literature. The attitude is exemplified by Petrarch's dictum: "There is only one important object of human thought, man himself,"[12] cutting Augustine's program at least by half. Pico detaches man from other beings as he is able to make himself to will what he will be, a theme taken up by Vives in his *Fabula de homine.*[13]

Kristeller indicates that the Renaissance brought no basic change in the methods and results of natural science.[14] However, it is possible that the Italian Aristotelians supplied a link to Galileo. Dame Frances Yates suggests that the scientific revolution was aborning and had two phases: "the first . . . consisting of an animistic universe operated by magic, the second . . . a mathematical universe operated by mechanics."[15] Touching upon the dark underside of the age, she suggests that the "hermetic training" of the imagination regarding the world helped to prepare the way for Descartes.

The Renaissance, insofar as philosophy is concerned, was an age of transition. It produced no thinkers of the very first order with the possible exception of Nicholas of Cusa. The speculative fireworks of Campa-

10. Burckhardt, *Civilization of the Renaissance,* 110.
11. Kristeller, *Studies in Renaissance Thought,* (1956), 1:265.
12. Petrarch, *Le Familiai,* IV, No. 1.
13. Kristeller, *Studies in Renaissance Thought,* 1:285.
14. Kristeller, *Studies in Renaissance Thought,* 1:12.
15. Frances A. Yates, *Giordano Bruno and the Hermetic Tradition* (Chicago: Univ. of Chicago Press, Midway reprint, 1979), 453.

nella and Bruno were no more than colorful and bizarre ephemera. The Aristotelians represented the hard core of professional philosophers, reigning at Bologna and later at Padua, but even they were not without links to the astrological and alchemical.[16] Pomponazzi (1462-1524), while paying lip service to Christian orthodoxy, maintained that the doctrine of immortality is contrary to natural principles. Religions are as transitory and fragile as individuals and morality is autonomous and self-contained. In this way he adumbrates Kant and opens the door to a purely secular morality.[17]

Platonism occupied a greater portion of the stage. Marsilio Ficino (1433-1499), a gifted and prolific translator, led the Platonic Academy of Florence, established by Cosimo de Medici and kept under the wing of the Medicis until 1494. In his principal work, the *Theologia Platonica*, Ficino places Platonic philosophy on the same authoritative level as Scripture while maintaining that it could be used to prop up Christianity. By this means, the faith "may be confirmed and rendered sufficiently rational to satisfy the skeptical and atheistical minds of the age."[18] He revives the ancient theory of innate ideas, later taken up by Descartes among others, and affirms the immortality of the soul. This is a truth, he states, confirmed not only by the philosophers but by the Persian sages and the Hermetic thinkers. With most Renaissance Platonists, Ficino affirms that the universe possesses an inner life, a unity that holds it together, systematically connecting all parts, a version of Plato's World Soul.[19]

Platonism proved to be the seedbed for the generation of utopias, fertilized by the Renaissance predilection for the spurious wisdom of Hermes Trismegistus's Egypt, the *Corpus Hermeticum*, which was taken very seriously indeed. It was considered to be the *prisca theologica*, the ancient theology which was both the source and confirmation of Plato's philosophy. It possessed the added attraction of resembling the inspired tones of

16. Kristeller, *Studies in Renaissance Thought*, 3:347.

17. Cited in *Renaissance Philosophy of Man*, 278. Cf. Kristellar, *Studies in Renaissance Thought*, 3:355.

18. Cited in *Renaissance Philosophy of Man*, 186-87.

19. Kristeller, *Studies in Renaissance Thought*, 3:13.

the book of Revelation. Cosimo de Medici had Ficino translate the *Corpus Hermeticum* prior to even the works of Plato. It was claimed that these works were able to provide the conditions for returning the world to its pristine beauty and restoring the golden age of Saturn.[20] This helped to stimulate the imagination and, together with backward glances at Plato's *Republic,* led to the creation of utopian lands of heart's desire.

St. Thomas More's *Utopia* appeared within the revolutionary hundred years that witnessed the discovery and conquest of the New World and the publication of Copernicus's *De revolutionibus.* It has been regarded, rightly so, as a masterpiece of Renaissance humanism.[21] In a letter to Erasmus, More refers to his work as *'Nusquamal,'* nowhere land. He coined the term "utopia" to the distress of later pedants, assuredly inspired by Plato's *Republic,* Book IX, where it is stated that the perfect republic exists only in discourse — in thought — not in concrete reality.[22] Through the mouth of his narrator, Rafael Hythlodeus, More proposes several novel ideas, opting for a republic, the abolition of property, and complete equality. The island community is composed of human beings as yet not seriously touched by religion and philosophy, held together by a form of natural law not exempt from restrictions: providence and immortality cannot be denied.[23]

More was a brilliant child of an exceptional time. He translated Lucan and cultivated music and the visual arts. Holbein lived for a while in his house. He opposed scholastic theology and seems to have believed that humanist scholarship, conscientiously applied to the Bible and the Fathers, would lead to a new improved version of religion.[24] His *Utopia* crystallized the urge for perfection undergirding the Renaissance. Distant and beckoning as a platonic idea, *Utopia* would exercise a powerful hold on the imagination of the West and initiate a long line of imagined utopias, from Campanella's *City of the Sun* to Bellamy's *Looking Backward,*

20. Yates, *Giordano Bruno,* 39-40; Kristellar, *Studies in Renaissance Thought,* 3:11.

21. Kristeller, *Studies in Renaissance Thought* (1982), 2:480.

22. Plato, *Republic* IX, 592aff.

23. Kristeller, *Studies in Renaissance Thought,* 2:480-83.

24. More, *Correspondence,* Nos. 15, 60, 75, 83. Cited by Kristellar, *Studies in Renaissance Thought,* 2:483-86.

and more. The residues of Joachimism, long underground, would surface in men such as Paracelsus annealed to hermetic lore. Paracelsus awaited the Age of the Holy Spirit, not as heightening of human spirituality, but as an era that would bring about the advance of the arts and sciences.

The hermetic is also present in Francis Bacon's *New Atlantis,* his utopia for technicians. Here, as Mumford indicates, Bacon "made the working partnership between science and technics an even more binding one by linking it to the immediate human desires for health, wealth, and power."[25] All discoveries and inventions are placed at the service of the community, ruled by an order called "Solomon's House," dedicated to study and research. Yet, behind the facade of hermeticism — the ruler riding in a chariot of gold burnished with a radiant sun, the symbol of Abraxas[26] — Bacon defines the project of modern technology by making it the ultimate justification of science. He initiates a movement that led to what Noble has called the "religion of technology."[27] A trivial example of the practical effect of utopias is afforded by Comenius's visit to England in an attempt to make Solomon's House a reality by founding scientific institutes. Later, the Protestant Reformer Johann Andreae's utopia, *Christianopolis,* required that the mechanical arts be practiced assiduously by its inhabitants.[28]

Tommasso Campanella enthusiastically greeted the new world inaugurated by Bacon and Galileo. To the latter he wrote that "the novelties of ancient truths, of new worlds, new systems, new nations, are the beginning of a new era."[29] He was born in Calabria, the region that produced Joachim of Fiore, by whose thought, usually at second remove, he was influenced. The imagination of the Renaissance reached a polychromatic plateau in his *Cittá del Sole* (City of the Sun). Campanella also predicted the advent of a new dispensation that would establish a superior religion

---

25. Mumford, *Pentagon of Power,* 2:160.

26. Yates, *Giordano Bruno,* 450.

27. David F. Noble, *The Religion of Technology* (New York: Alfred A. Knopf, 1997), 49, 54.

28. Noble, *Religion of Technology,* 41.

29. Cited by Mumford, *Pentagon of Power,* 2:13.

and a superior morality both grounded on nature.[30] An agitated spirit, he organized a revolt against Spanish rule in 1598, believing that it would pave the way for the New Age that would be organized politically as a republic.

The topography of the City of the Sun reproduces the seven tiers or circles of Zoharic Kabbalah, a scheme also employed by Sta. Teresa de Jesus in her *Interior Castle*. Here, the seven subdivisions or *giri* correspond to the seven planets. In the center, on the summit of a hill, was placed an altar with two gigantic *mapamundi* depicting the heavens and the earth, presided over by a Sun-Priest. Everything is held in common. Brotherly love prevails. Dame Frances Yates relates this utopia to hermetic writings:

> To my mind, the closest parallel to Campanella's *City of the Sun* is none other than the City of Adocentyn in *Picatrix*[31] in which Hermes is stated to have been the first to use magic images and that he founded a marvellous city in Egypt.[32]

Although the Joachite influence is present, found mainly in his language and trinitarian symbolism, this utopia propounds a cult of nature, of the world, of a universe in which Christ is absent. Power is succeeded by Wisdom, and Wisdom is followed by Love. The reign of Love is about to dawn.[33] This version of the Age of the Holy Spirit will have profound resonance in the thought of Lessing, Saint-Simon, and Auguste Comte.

From the twilight of the Renaissance emerged the bizarre figure of Giordano Bruno. He was quite possibly, as Yates believes him to be, an out-and-out magician for whom Copernican heliocentricity heralded the return of magical religion.[34] Through his hermetic interpretation of

30. Yates, *Giordano Bruno*, 364.

31. The *Picatrix* is a treatise on sympathetic and astral magic, with particular reference to talismans. Though not assigned to Hermes Trismegistus, it mentions him with great respect. It was originally written in Arabic, probably in the twelfth century AD.

32. Yates, *Giordano Bruno*, 54, 370.

33. Frank E. Manuel, *Shapes of Philosophical History* (Stanford: Stanford Univ. Press, 1965), 43.

34. Yates, *Giordano Bruno*, 451.

Lucretius and Copernicus, Bruno arrived at a numbing vision of the infinite extension of the divine as it is reflected in nature: an innumerable number of worlds moving like gigantic beasts, populating an infinite universe. Bruno's luxuriant fantasy at times approximated scientific insight. Often it did not. He also surmised that the "new heaven" and the "new earth" signified that the moon and planets were inhabited, and suggested in his *Apologia pro Galileo* that paradise was located on the moon.[35]

It is hardly necessary to review the novel, bizarre, and radical ideas elaborated during the Renaissance to conclude that the medieval world-vision of Christendom had been shattered. The search for the unique, the grand, the gigantic, the splendid, and the outrageous at the service of perfervid imagination caused a radical upset. The cult of unfettered passion and will led to the substitution of holiness by *magnanitá,* superlative greatness. The fabric of tradition was corroded by indulgence in the spectacular, an avalanche of gilded trivia, from banquets capped by fantastic interludes *(intermezzi)* to menageries *(seragli)*, often featuring human beings.[36] One intermezzi given at Florence on the election of Pope Leo X represented the Ages of the World: five scenes of Roman history were followed by two allegories of the golden age of Saturn and its final return.[37] History, its speculation lost to the age, as was the tragic muse, surfaced as entertainment.

Christianity survived — albeit in a weakened form, fragmented by the Reformation — in customs, mores, and traditions, in the hearts of the common people and residually present in the minds of even the most radical thinkers. Moreover, the Fathers, especially Augustine, still retained substantial authority.[38] It did not escape the Humanists that Augustine (and other Fathers) were imbued with classical learning, that they were, as Erasmus noted, *grammatici*.[39] Both Vives and Erasmus

35. Marjorie Hope Nicholson, *Voyages to the Moon* (New York: Macmillan, 1948), 20, 27.

36. Burckhardt, *Civilization of the Renaissance,* 191.

37. Burckhardt, *Civilization of the Renaissance,* 267-68.

38. Kristeller, *Studies in Renaissance Thought,* 1:360.

39. Kristeller, *Studies in Renaissance Thought,* 1:363.

published critical editions of Augustine's works, the former's edition of the *City of God* dedicated to King Henry VIII. Petrarch's *Secretum* consists of a dialogue between himself and Augustine. Ficino cites him with regularity. Nicholas of Cusa was familiar with Augustine's works to the extent of borrowing the term *docta ignorantia,* the title of his most important work.[40]

Oddly, the account which comes closest to philosophy of history was provided by Montaigne (1533-1592) and attributed to the New World. Standing at the end of the era, Montaigne preserved many characteristic traits of the Renaissance — naturalism, a cultivated cynicism, a taste for the heterodox and for reflectiveness, as well as an incredibly defective memory.[41] The account was taken from Francisco López de Gomara's *History of the Indies.*

The "Mexicans" believed that the duration of the world is divided into five ages, each age corresponding to the life of a sun. Four ages have been traversed and the Spanish *conquista* augurs the demise of the fifth: the end of the world. The previous ages perished in different ways. The first perished because of a universal flood, the second by the sky crashing to the earth, the third by fire. The fourth was the most eventful, perishing by a great turbulence which leveled mountains and transformed human beings into apes. The world was then plunged into darkness for twenty-five years, in the fifteenth of which a man and woman were created, thus restoring the human race. In the twenty-fifth year the sun was recreated. Three days later the gods died and new gods were born *seriatim.*[42] This seems to be an exotic pastiche with Christian elements coming from the good Friar.

Post-Renaissance Christianity was divided, weakened, and secularized. However, among those traditional elements that survived and rose to the surface after hibernation was the conception of time as linear. History and speculation as to the manner of its unfolding again

---

40. Kristeller, *Studies in Renaissance Thought,* 1:366-67; 2:475.

41. Michel de Montaigne, *Essays,* trans. J. M. Cohen (London: Penguin, 1988), I, 26; II, 17 et al. (pp. 28, 83, 159, 212-13).

42. Montaigne, *Essays,* III, 6 (pp. 283-84). Cf. Laurette Sejourne, *Burning Water* (London: Thames and Hudson, 1957).

came to the fore. The philosophy of history recovered its wings with Bishop Bossuet looking backward, taking his inspiration from Augustine, and Giambattista Vico, looking forward to regions as yet unexplored.

CHAPTER 6

Bossuet and Vico:
The Doorway to Modernity

E urope weathered the Renaissance only to enter the crucible of the Reformation and emerge weakened and divided. Protestantism acknowledged the primacy of Scripture while rejecting the authority of Peter, ecclesiastical hierarchy, monastic spirituality, and the rationalization of belief represented by scholasticism. However, as early as 1526, Luther stated that books on logic, rhetoric, and poetics would prove useful for the education of youth. Melanchthon wrote several manuals of Aristotelian inspiration, the first in 1520, entitled *Compendiaria Dialectices Ratio.* Osiander was favorably disposed towards the Copernican system.

The mathematization of nature advanced by Galileo began to make inroads even in the universities where the residue of Aristotelian thought still reigned supreme. Only with the philosophies of Descartes and Leibniz would the Peripatetic hold on the schools begin to weaken. Insofar as speculation on history is concerned, Francis Bacon had already divided history into *historia civilis* and *historia naturalis,* including the history of philosophy under the former. Thomas Hobbes (1588-1679), in regular communication with Gassendi and Mersenne and favoring the theories of Copernicus, Kepler, and Galileo, translated Thucydides into English with the express purpose of inculcating fear of democracy.

René Descartes (1596-1650), Baruch Spinoza (1632-1677), and Gottfried Wilhelm von Leibniz (1646-1710) inaugurated modern philosophy on a serious note. Descartes' *Meditationes de Prima Philosophia* initiated a current of such richness that it was resuscitated three centuries later as the inspiration for Husserl's *Cartesian Meditations,* itself designed to inspire another new beginning of philosophy in phenomenology. Descartes' *cogito* opened a Pandora's box that has yet to be fully exploited. Spinoza's speculations, as presented in his *Ethics,* rejected traditional creation, subtlety obviated by his distinction between *natura naturans* and *natura naturata.* This led to a denial of history in the strict sense of the term. Nevertheless, his *Tractatus Theologico-Politicus,* in line with Hobbes's dictum that Scripture be interpreted by the same method as nature, influenced scriptural criticism to a great extent. Leibniz constructed an ironclad system parcelled out in time in which the death rattle of the last man is already present in the concept of Adam. Novelty is eliminated. In spite of his Christian faith and status as a historian, Leibniz's philosophy did not exercise a great influence on speculation concerning history except in the case of Gotthold Lessing (1729-1781).

The historical muse again spread its wings in the writings of Bishop Bossuet (1627-1704) and Giambattista Vico (1668-1744). It was a time when England was on the rise; France, under King Louis XIV, was successfully vying with Spain for the mastership of Europe, and Holland was building an empire in the Far East. The ancient kingdom of Naples, the home of Vico, was under the rule of the Spanish Crown, as it had been for generations.

Bossuet was acclaimed as a superb preacher and elegant stylist who raised the *oraison funèbre* to heights heretofore unequalled in France. Sermons such as "Sur la Mort," "Sur la Justice," and "Sur L'amour des Plaisirs" made him the paladin of oratory.[1] His principal work, the *Discours sur L'Histoire Universelle,* was ostensibly written for the instruction of the Dauphin, the son of Louis XIV, as was also an insightful manual, the *Connaissance de Dieu et de Soi-Même,* touching on such disparate themes as logic, free will, and politics.[2]

Although Bossuet attempted to emulate Augustine and, to a great ex-

1. *Bossuet: A Prose Anthology,* ed. J. Standring (London: George C. Harrap & Co. Ltd., 1962), 20ff.

2. Bossuet, *Prose Anthology,* 33.

tent, follow in his footsteps, he parted company on several points. To begin with, he was more interested in history per se. As Lowith has indicated, "compared with the *City of God,* the *Discours* of Bossuet shows a greater historical sense for the grandeur of political history and a greater interest in the pragmatic concatenation of causes and effects."[3] His major theme: Providence as the guide of world history. Bossuet attempts to counter the errors of "atheists" and "immoralists" who interpret the apparent disorder manifested in history as a denial of Divine Wisdom, disguising it as a type of spiritual astigmatism. History, when contemplated at a greater distance and with the eyes of faith, reveals a hidden justice at work. Particular designs can conflict — be opposed or upset — but "the all-embracing design of God cannot be upset."[4] Temporal events cooperate in the fulfillment of Providence's eternal purpose.

Comparing Bossuet and Augustine, Bossuet's emphasis does not center on the *Civitas Dei* but, after the manner of Eusebius, on the history of the church triumphant. This is borne out by the very structure of the *Discours.* The first part provides a general outline of the twelve epochs and seven ages of the world without making any distinction between sacred and profane events, in effect conflating sacred and secular history. Nevertheless, he does mark the great watershed which divides world history as the birth of Christ, the year 1. Other key dates are 4004 BC, the date of creation; 754 BC, the foundation of Rome; and those corresponding to the twelve epochs. The seventh age, inaugurated by the birth of Christ, is the last. It will perdure until the EndTime.

The second part of the *Discours* deals with the history of religion as centered on the Old Testament Hebrews, the third with the history of empires. Bossuet indicates that the *Civitas Dei* extends from Abraham to the church victorious, the *Civitas Terrena* from Egypt to the Roman Empire.[5] Although the two cities are distinct, he does not preclude their eventual merger: "They run together in that great movement of ages, where they have . . . one and the same course."[6] For Bossuet the ultimate

3. Karl Lowith, *Meaning in History* (Chicago: Univ. of Chicago Press, 1949), 138.
4. Cited in Lowith, *Meaning in History,* 138.
5. Lowith, *Meaning in History,* 139.
6. Bossuet, *Discours,* I, 12.

meaning of the entire course of history depends on the relation of *historia sacra* and *historia profana,* of sacred to secular history, both of which have a religious foundation. The history of the "chosen people" is the most patent manifestation of Divine Providence and illustrates uniquely their religious underpinning. Other instances are not lacking, perhaps the most prominent being the convergence of the Pax Romana under Augustus and the birth of Jesus Christ, the first the necessary prerequisite for the expansion of the gospel.[7]

The empires of the world minister unwittingly to religion and the preservation of the people of God, the church. This "new holy people" constitutes an empire: "the empire of the son of man, the empire that is to stand amidst the ruin of all others, and to which alone eternity is promised."[8]

In the last chapter of the *Discours,* Bossuet again takes up the theme of a Providence that imposes an orderly design on events, which, to the unspiritual eye, appear to be no more than a mixture of chance and fate. Everything ministers to designs higher than its own. In Lowith's words: "God only knows how to bring everything about to his will: therefore, everything is 'surprising' if only particular causes are considered; and yet everything goes on with a regular progression."[9]

This principle adumbrates a vision that will later emerge as Hegel's "cunning of reason" and generate a number of variations. Bossuet, always the prudent churchman, advises that this concordance should hardly be considered a boon as only *post festum* is Providence intelligible. It should be kept in mind that the Son of God died without any visible sign of divine protection. We should not claim for ourselves a privilege that was not granted to Christ. The only mark of election to the Christian is the cross.[10]

Very much a moralist, Bossuet was at his combative best when attacking "libertines," Protestants, and Jews, although, in the last two cases, charity soon took the place of ire. He denounced the "libertines," censuring their pride, lack of moderation, self-imposed imbecility, and the absurdities they embraced, especially targeting the plays of Molière. In his

7. Lowith, *Meaning in History,* 140
8. Bossuet, *Discours,* II, 20-21; III, 1.
9. Lowith, *Meaning in History,* 142.
10. Lowith, *Meaning in History,* 143-44.

funeral oration for Ana de Gonzaga (1685), Bossuet fingers the cause of their errors: their subjection to and advocacy of Nature. In the *Discours* the God of Spinoza *(Deus sive Natural),* chained to the laws of nature, is compared to Moses' God, the creator of the world, its absolute *seignor.* Bossuet censures even such well-meaning philosophers as Malebranche, who "accommodate the plans of God to their thought . . . as if the Sovereign Intelligence could not comprehend particular things."[11]

The avant-propos of the *Discours* can be studied with profit. Bossuet indicates that there are two things which impress themselves forcibly on our memory. They are religion and empires, "the two points around which things human revolve and which disclose the order and progression of mankind."[12] In this way it is possible to observe the succession of empires and contemplate the perpetual duration of religion. This is reflected in his account of the twelve epochs, which, unlike the seven ages, does not follow a traditional scheme.

The epochs begin, very logically, with (1) Adam or creation; then (2) Noah or the deluge; (3) Abraham or the beginning of man's alliance with God; (4) Moses or the written law. It then crosses into secular history with (5) the conquest of Troy; only to return to sacred history in (6) Solomon or the foundation of the Temple; again crossing to secular history in (7) Romulus or the foundation of Rome; (8) Cyrus or deliverance from the Babylonian captivity; (9) Scipio or Carthage vanquished. In (10) the birth of Jesus Christ, he proceeds to meld the sacred and secular; (11) Constantine or the Peace of the Church; (12) Charlemagne or the establishment of the New Empire.[13] Very much a mixed company with the last epoch marking the end of ancient history as well as the beginning of the French monarchy of which Bossuet was an ardent supporter.

If Bossuet attacked the immoralists, on a more theoretical level he viewed Descartes and Cartesianism with hostility. This philosophy, he in-

11. Cited by Jacques Chevalier, *Historia del Pensamiento,* trans. Jose Antonio Miguez (Madrid: Aguilar, 1963), 3:397.
12. *Selections from Bossuet,* trans. C. H. C. Wright (New York: Oxford Univ. Press, 1930), 84-85; 86-87.
13. *Selections from Bossuet.*

dicated, would prove to be noxious. Heresies would inevitably arise from its fundamental principles. Descartes' criterion of clear and distinct ideas leads to hubris, promotes a false sense of freedom, and rejects much that is undoubtedly valuable. This mode of thinking is able to generate an "occult pleasure" which tempts man to elevate himself above religion by transforming himself into a god. This dislike of Cartesianism became standard coinage with most advocates of a philosophy of history. Moreover, Bossuet feared that a state of anarchy was approaching, disguised under the façade of Nature and Reason. His reply to this aberration of the spirit would influence the entire eighteenth century: "Anarchy cannot delegate sovereignty."[14]

The work of Providence is attested to by the antiquity of religion: "Its continued existence without interruption and without alteration during so many ages, and in spite of so many intervening obstacles, made manifest the sustaining hand of God."[15] From the very beginning religion is anchored in God, a powerful God, infinitely superior to the 'first cause' and 'first mover' of the philosophers, whose power is made manifest in creation. The overarching direction of Providence should not lead to a naive optimism. Humanity, because of the Fall, retains an 'eternal impression' of divine vengeance. The vestiges of ancient concord, reflected in a common language, were lost and, as Bossuet states in a trenchant phrase, "death advances with hurried steps."[16] Ignorance and spiritual blindness burgeon. While the Hebrews remained the depositories of truth, the Gentiles worshipped beasts and reptiles: "Everything was God except God Himself."[17]

The Mosaic Law, which Bossuet places in the company of the laws of Romulus, Numa, and the Twelve Tables (Rome), Solon (Athens), and Lycurgus (Sparta), prepared the way for the Messiah. Jerusalem was the image and preparation of the church. The Old Testament prophets initiate a process which comes to a head in Jesus Christ, the "master of mankind," the "pattern of perfection," who brings into being a new order of

14. *Selections from Bossuet;* Chevalier, *Historia,* 397. Refer to Mousnier, *Siècle XVII,* 349.

15. Bossuet, *The Continuity of Religion* (Second Part of the *Discours*), trans. Victor Day (Helena: V. Day, 1930), 5.

16. Bossuet, *Continuity,* 16, 18.

17. Bossuet, *Continuity,* 32, 36.

things. With the words spoken from the cross, "It is consummated," Jesus expires and "everything changes in the world; the law ceases, its figures pass away . . . all nature is moved."[18] The prophecies of Isaiah and St. Paul regarding the conversion of the Gentiles and the return of the Jews move towards fulfillment.

The special vocation of the Hebrews is passed on to the Apostles and the church, which is immune to destruction: "the work of God has stood fast and the Church has triumphed over idolatry and all error."[19]

In his own day, Bossuet censured Malebranche's *Treatise on Nature and Grace* (1680) as *"pulchra, nova, falsa"* yet joined with him in the acrimonious disputation over quietism.[20] The seventeenth century drew to a close with a bitter debate between Bossuet, who supported the divine right of kings, and Jurieu, the Protestant statesman, who defended the sovereignty of the people.[21] He became the leader of the Gallican party, which supported Louis XIV in his disputes with the Papacy, and worked for the revocation of the Edict of Nantes. He left four principal works and some two hundred sermons and panegyrics.

Although his reputation as writer and orator grew with the passing of time, Bossuet has been vilified almost as much as he has been praised. In a bizarre about-face, he was attacked by De Maistre and praised by Saint-Simon. Fairly recently, Manuel dismissed the *Discours* as a "travesty," a "sterile caricature" of Augustine's providential history.[22] No doubt Bossuet's intellectual gifts were wildly inferior to those of Augustine. No doubt the *Discours* marks a fissure in the seamless garment of the Two Cities: the *Civitas Dei* is equated with the church — resonances of Otto von Freising — and the church immured in the slough of secular history.

Despite this, Bishop Bossuet can be credited with restoring speculation on the course of history to prominence. This he did with ecclesiasti-

---

18. Bossuet, *Continuity*, 97, 100.

19. Bossuet, *Continuity*, 193.

20. Emile Bréhier, *The History of Philosophy: The Seventeenth Century*, trans. Wade Baskin (1938; Chicago: Univ. of Chicago Press, 1968), 197-98.

21. Bréhier, *Seventeenth Century*, 3.

22. Frank E. Manuel, *Shapes of Philosophical History* (Stanford: Stanford Univ. Press, 1965), 34.

cal gravity and literary elegance. He broke new ground by including the *Civitas Terrena* within the march of the *Civitas Dei*. This prepared the way for Vico, who would take the further step of excluding, at least in the practical order, the *Civitas Dei* from the course of secular history while elaborating a philosophy of history notably lacking in eschatological fiber. Bossuet stands at the doorway to modernity.

Giambattista Vico was born in Naples of a large family in modest circumstances in June 1668. Fortune did not pursue him except perhaps posthumously. As a youth he fractured his head. Complications ensued to the point where his surgeon predicted that Vico would either die or lapse into idiocy. Later he acquired the name of *'Mastro Tisicuzzo'* (Mr. Skin & Bones) because of his delicate health.[23] Vico went on to marry a good but illiterate woman, Teresa Destito, who would bear a brood of children, one of which showed evidence of pathological behavior. Although he obtained a modest Chair of Rhetoric at the University of Naples, he failed in his bid for the prestigious Chair of Civil Law, a post for which he was eminently qualified. His great work, the *Scienza Nuova,* was greeted with a chilling indifference. Cardinal Lorenzo Corsini, to whom the work was dedicated, withdrew his offer of subsidizing its printing. In addition, two volumes that would have acted as prolegomena to the *Scienza* were lost.[24] Only towards the end of his life, the length and productivity of which gave the lie to his surgeon's prediction, did Vico receive a well-deserved honor. After the restoration of Spanish rule Vico was appointed Historiographer Royal. He died in 1744.

Vico wrote four major works: *De Ratione Studiorum* (1708), *De Antiquissima Italorum Sapientia* (1710), *Jus Universale* (1720), and the *Principii di Scienza Nuova* (1722). He wrote many orations and panegyrics — often comically fawning[25] — and was something of a poet, a genre

---

23. H. P. Adams, *The Life and Writings of Giambattista Vico* (London: Allen & Unwin, 1935), 16. Benedetto Croce, *The Philosophy of Giambattista Vico,* trans. R. G. Collingwood (1913; New York: Russell & Russell, 1964), Appendix I, p. 254.

24. Adams, *Life and Writings,* 142-44.

25. A good example is Vico's reference to Philip V as the greatest being on earth who in his royal body was more beautiful than a beautiful woman. Adams, *Life and Writings,* 84.

in which he was able to express his feelings. The *Affeto di un Disperato,* considered his best poem, appeals to heaven to continue battering him with hardships, to experience nothing but bitter suffering.[26] It is fortunate that his historical speculations took a less emotional turn.

Vico was an ardent admirer of Plato and Tacitus, although he believed that Plato's *Republic* was defective because of his ignorance of the first man's fall.[27] He studied assiduously the "philologists" (historians) of ancient Rome and medieval Italy and was captivated by the "mighty torrent" of Dante. Like Bossuet, he reacted against Cartesian philosophy and Galileo's mathematization of nature.[28] Vico believed that Descartes' "methodical doubt" limps toward only a "tiny piece" of certain truth. Insofar as mathematics is concerned, it is a human construct related only tenuously to the physical world, which itself is only the less significant half of reality.[29]

His 1708 oration targets Cartesianism, which he takes to task for disregarding everything except the absolute truth for which it provides the criterion, neglecting civil wisdom, eloquence, and art. In applying the mathematical, which is to say the geometrical method, it arrives only at a purely formal truth. In addition, the *cogito* does not provide knowledge of our existence but only consciousness of it. And to arrive at consciousness of our existence, philosophy is hardly required. *A priori* reasoning is not only erroneous, it is blasphemous. Vico makes a trenchant attack on the *a priori* demonstrations for the existence of God. They amount to making its propounder the god of God and hence "to deny the God they seek."[30]

Why is this so? It is because real knowledge is knowledge through causes. We can know thoroughly only that which we have caused or made. The true is identical with the made or *factum.* As Collingwood states: "It follows from the *Verum = Factum* principle that history, which is something made by the human mind, is especially adapted to be an object of human knowledge."[31] In this manner, Vico is attempting to establish

26. Adams, *Life and Writings,* 43.
27. Croce, *Philosophy,* 106.
28. Adams, *Life and Writings,* 40ff.
29. Lowith, *Meaning in History,* 119.
30. Adams, *Life and Writings,* 89f., 92, 95.
31. R. G. Collingwood, *The Idea of History* (New York: Oxford Univ. Press, 1956), 65.

the philosophy of history as a science independent of mathematics, in fact, as the science *par excellence.* Philosophy becomes the outcome of history, and history is rescued from its condition of inferiority. To do so he was obliged to launch this attack on Descartes and the mathematization of nature, which had monopolized the intellectual horizon of the age.

In his biography of Marshal Caraffa, Vico cites with approval the Marshal's dictum that the characters of men are formed by the institutions under which they live: "Minds are formed by language, not language by minds."[32] He arrived at the conclusion that a serious study of history must be partly pre-historic — a search for origins — and partly metaphysical — a search for universal principles.[33] Although the 'world of nature', ruled by inflexible law and displaying supreme order, is in some way superior to the 'world of man', a veritable spectacle of weakness and confusion, it is the latter which is in the full sense, a science.

The title of the third edition of Vico's *New Science,* which appeared in July 1744, was *Principles of the New Science of Giambattista Vico Concerning the Common Nature of the Nations.*[34] The latter part merits discussion. What is a 'nation', a 'common nature'? To Vico, etymologically a nation is a 'birth', a 'being born'. The *"mondo delle nazioni"* (world of nations) is a system, an order created out of chaos, out of the confusion of Noah's non-Hebraic descendants. Vico allows a period of about two centuries to intervene between the creation of man and humanity lapsing into a bestial state.[35] The 'world of nations' then begins to be born, having its origins in the primitive institutions of religion, marriage, and burial, out of which the entire complex of social institutions developed.

The 'world of nations' where the New Science holds court is the *Civitas Terrena.* Each nation experiences the progressive appearance of three natures, the Divine, the Heroic, and the Human, the acme and term of the process. The Human is "the true and proper nature of man."[36] The 'com-

32. Adams, *Life and Writings,* 105.

33. Adams, *Life and Writings,* 113.

34. Giambattista Vico, *The New Science of Giambattista Vico* (1744), trans. Thomas Goddard Bergin and Max Harold Fisch (Garden City: Doubleday Anchor, 1961), xxi.

35. Vico, *New Science,* #377, 379, 688, 725.

36. Vico, *New Science,* #924, 973.

mon nature' is its point of origin. A complete absence of structure prevails. It is a state of chaos, of promiscuity. This is illustrated by Vico's understanding of 'common sense' as "judgment without reflection shared by an entire class . . . people . . . nations . . . or human race."[37] This race of bestial commonness, of men-beasts, humanizes itself by means of the primitive institutions (religion, marriage, and burial) and prods the civilizational process into motion.

Following "ancient Egyptian tradition" Vico postulates the existence of three ages, which succeed each other seriatim: the Divine, the Heroic, and the Human. The first age is theocratic, the second mythological, and the third rational. Starting from a condition of brutish simplicity in which even language was not yet developed, the proto-human begins to humanize himself through the medium of religion, which originates in fear, itself the origin of shame, mother of all the virtues.[38] Fear of natural phenomena leads to settled habitation and this, in turn, leads to marriage and the burial of the dead. Fugitives in search of protection then accost the settled families. Protection is granted. The Divine Age, the Age of the Gods, comes to an end. The Age of Heroes begins.

Society becomes a clan composed of aristocrats (the 'heroes') and plebeians (the protected fugitives). When the plebeians begin to claim rights, aristocrats band together under a leader. He becomes their first king. However, the plebeians, who represent reason, strive against the aristocrats, representing authority, to attain full *'humanitas'* and ultimately bring about the vindication of the rational nature of man as such. The Age of Men succeeds the Age of the Heroes. The process does not end but reverses itself, as this third age inevitably generates a "humanization of customs" that leads to decadence and collapse. Civilization comes to an end with a whimper in the contemptible barbarism of reflection. The *corso* (flux) comes to its term and the *recorso* (reflux) begins, which entails a return to the chaotic but wild and noble barbarism of sensation.

According to Vico the authentic Republic is not the abstract creation of Plato but rather the entire course of history with brutes at one end of

37. Vico, *New Science,* #142.
38. Vico, *New Science,* #31; Croce, *Philosophy,* 83.

the spectrum and Plato at the other. History itself is the *"generis humani respublicae."*[39] Its course, its movement, its articulation, is regulated by Providence. In Croce's words, "from this point of view the New Science may be defined as a rational civil theology of the divine providence."[40] It must be emphasized that Vico's providence is not the miraculous, transcendent providence of Bossuet. It begins to work in primitive man through 'natural law' by means of an inchoate belief that becomes progessively more explicit. It is instituted in separate regions, each in ignorance of the others, and only subsequently does it come to be recognized as common to the human race.[41]

Vico makes an important distinction between *coscienza* (consciousness), which has as its object *il certo* (the certain), and *scienza* (knowledge), which has as its object *il vero* (the true). The certain deals with the individual and particular (facts, events, customs, laws, etc.) while the true deals with the common, universal, and eternal principles. Vico often uses *scienza* in a liberal sense, embracing both history and philosophy. This is because the philosophers erred by failing to anchor their arguments to certainty; the historians by not providing their authority with the sanction of truth.[42] Vico's New Science is superior to physics in being complete and superior to mathematics in being real.[43] History is a process of unfolding, of ebb and flow. While God alone can know the 'world of nature', knowledge of the 'world of nations' can be known to man as its principles are encountered within the modifications of the human mind.

The point of departure for this science, its "master key," the principle of the origin of both letters and language, lies in the fact that the early

39. Croce, *Philosophy,* 108.
40. Croce, *Philosophy,* 112.
41. Vico, *New Science,* #398, 146. This notion of Natural Law is to be distinguished from the classic formulation of St. Thomas Aquinas: a participation in the Eternal Law by the rational creature in which his activity is inclined toward its appropriate end. *Summa Theologica,* 1-2, 91, 2; 96, 2 ad 1; 97.1 ad 1. Vico, however, does distinguish between natural law *(diritto)* and positive law *(legge)*.
42. Vico, *New Science,* #138ff.
43. Vico, *New Science,* #331, 349.

Gentiles were poets in the Greek sense of "makers" or "creators" and spoke in poetic characters.[44] Poetry, Vico urges, is the primary activity of the human mind produced by natural necessity. In this 'poetic wisdom' the very crude beginnings of the arts and sciences can be discerned.[45] From this 'wisdom' also proceed the principles of religion, marriage, and burial, which generate a 'minimal society' — one that outlives its members — and provide the basis on which society still preserves itself.[46]

Vico delights in triads. This recalls Joachim of Fiore and adumbrates Hegel. This characteristic division, which commences with the three ages, is applied to customs, language, natural law, governments, character jurisprudence, authority, and reason, all hanging on the three types of human nature that succeed each other. As Vico indicates, "the nations will be seen to develop in conformity with this division, by a constant and uninterrupted order of causes and effects present in every nation through three kinds of natures."[47]

In sum, all phenomena follow the movement of the three ages, the ebb and flow of *corso* and *recorso*. It may appear that Vico is regressing to the cyclical theories of antiquity but such a move was precluded by his fervent, albeit idiosyncratic, Catholicism. The final statement of the *Scienza Nuova,* which commentators affirm should be taken seriously, states that "this Science carries inseparably with it the study of piety, and that he who is not pious cannot be truly wise."[48] Croce, however, while admitting the complete sway that Catholicism held over Vico, indicates that he invariably reduced the transcendent to the immanent and this implicitly contained a criticism of Christian transcendence.[49]

Due in part to this theological ambivalence, Vico's theory is more of a spiral than a circle. Although man makes history, it is providence which organizes and guides it. The providence which is dimly perceived by primitive man and leads to the constitution of the *mondo civile* is but a

44. Vico, *New Science,* #34.
45. Vico, *New Science,* #365, 391, 661, 734.
46. Vico, *New Science,* #330-37.
47. Vico, *New Science,* #916ff.
48. Vico, *New Science,* #1112.
49. Croce, *Philosophy,* pp. 21, 117, Appendix I, pp. 247-48.

shadow of the Providence that creates — God. Yet it is the immanent providence, close at hand, which can be perceived as the organizing principle of human society and undergirds the preservation of the human race.[50] With some justification Peters affirms that "nothing remains of the transcendent and miraculous operation which characterizes faith in providence from Augustine to Bossuet."[51] Vico is silent concerning the status of Jesus Christ as the unique watershed of history. He all but eliminates the Bible as a historical source. How can this be explained?

The New Science deals with the 'world of nations', which is structured by the immanent providence. It is able to chart the movement of history without appealing to transcendent revelation. God remains the object of faith but only providence, his immanent surrogate, is an object of reason. The biblical tradition is bracketed: the Old Testament Hebrews are excluded from the laborious trek towards full humanity that characterizes the 'Gentile' nations. They are created fully human. Christian theology is viewed as a mixture of the "loftiest revealed theology" and the "civil theology" of the ancients. He views the Christian Middle Ages as an example of the *ricorso,* the ebb of history, a second heroic barbarism, annealed this time by the "true religion."

In any case, the *Civitas Dei* is decidedly an aberration to be excluded from the mapped-out world of the *Civitas Terrena.* The New Science lacks an eschatological finale. The three ages, the ebb and flow, repeat themselves interminably . . . as long as the civil world remains in existence. Hannah Arendt suggests that it is "only modern technology (and no mere science, no matter how highly developed), which began with substituting mechanical process for human activities — laboring and working — and ended with starting new natural processes, which would have been wholly adequate to Vico's ideal of knowledge."[52] Under modern conditions Vico would have turned to technology not to history. This is an ingenious hypothesis which, however, appears to miss the point.

Überweg was not unduly exaggerating when he expressed the view

50. Vico, *New Science,* #344, 1108.

51. Cited in Lowith, *Meaning in History,* 123. Peters, *Der Aufbau des Weltgeschichte bei Vico* (Berlin, 1929), ch. 7.

52. Hannah Arendt, *Between Past and Future* (1961; New York: Penguin, 1993), 51-52.

that Vico was the founder of the philosophy of history.[53] Recently, Lowith credited him with providing the first empirical construction of universal history.[54] Vico can also be considered as effecting the transition from the theology to the philosophy of history, as in his thought the theological aspect, though present, is something of an intruder. It must be allowed that, possibly in spite of himself, Vico initiates a process of secularization which will influence greatly the evolution of the discipline. More important, he justified history as a science and muted the overpowering inclination of philosophers of history — encountered later in Comte — of attempting to model their speculations on mathematics. Nevertheless, Molnar indicates that Vico rehabilitated the idea of the universe as a meaningless flux in which meaning is derived only from humanity. Man is the master, not the servant, of religion as he is able, by reformulating the basic institutions (religion, marriage, and burial), to reshape his social environment.[55]

Vico's influence was substantial in Italy, where his thought cut a swath from minor figures such as Filangeri, Foscolo, and Janelli, to major thinkers such as Rosmini, Gioberti, Gentile, and Croce. In France he exercised an influence on Montesquieu even before Michelet (1827) translated the *Scienza Nuova*. He was read and admired by Comte, influenced the theories of Fustel de Coulanges, and even struck a spark in Spain, where Donoso Cortés commented on his work. While Vico was not known to Hegel, his thought anticipated that of Herder, Dilthey, Spengler, and others. With Vico, the philosophy of history passed the threshold of the modern world.

53. Friedrich Überweg, *History of Philosophy,* trans. George S. Morris (New York: Charles Scribner's Sons, 1873), 2:473; Addenda, p. 523.

54. Lowith, *Meaning in History,* 116.

55. Thomas Molnar, *The Pagan Temptation* (Grand Rapids: Eerdmans, 1987), pp. 109, 118-19.

CHAPTER 7

Hegel — History as Providence Transfigured

Nietzsche began an early unpublished essay, "On Truth and Lie in an Extra-Moral Sense" with a parable. A clever animal living on an obscure planet invents knowledge. Pursuing this knowledge, he ultimately discovers his own and his planet's extinction.[1] A superb illustration of this parable is afforded by the career of the philosophy of history from the Enlightenment to the present. This movement is initiated by the Enlightenment which, as Berdyaev has indicated, attacked and attempted to discredit the sacred in the historical and all the organic and traditional elements of history.[2] Christian dogma and symbolism were transmuted into secular analogues, parasites deriving vitality from their host. The pursuit of autonomy, the abolition of all limitations, masquerading as freedom, dominated the age. Optimism, Romanticism, and confusion set their seal on historical speculation. Kant, Herder, Lessing, Fichte, and Schelling prepared the way for the culmination of this movement in the thought of G. W. F. Hegel.[3]

---

1. Cited by Lawrence Lambert, *Leo Strauss and Nietzsche* (Chicago: Univ. of Chicago Press, 1996), 52.

2. Nicholas Berdyaev, *The Meaning of History,* trans. George Reavey (Cleveland: Meridian, 1962), 18-19.

3. "The culmination of the historical movement which began in 1784 with Herder came with Hegel, whose Lectures on the Philosophy of History were first delivered in 1822-1823." R. G. Collingwood, *The Idea of History* (New York: Oxford Univ. Press, 1956),

Immanuel Kant (1724-1804) was influenced by Rousseau and his romantic ideology. History replaced nature as the privileged domain of reality. The notion of progress begins to make an appearance. Freedom was stressed as a human prerogative. Kant praised the French and American Revolutions as they realized the idea of political freedom. In this spirit, he reduced religion to morality and dogma to ethical doctrine: "The truly religious spirit is that which recognizes all our duties as divine commands."[4] The 'Kingdom of God' approaches, its proximity evidenced by the gradual transition taking place from 'ecclesiastical faith' to 'purely religious faith' grounded in reason. Kant looked forward to the day when man is considered to be the rational world in its complete moral purification. On reaching this point, man may be figuratively represented as the Son of God.[5]

Eschatology is replaced by the 'kingdom of ends' as an actuality,[6] a corollary to Kant's belief in the renovation of humanity through its employment of freedom. His 'Kingdom of God' includes the totality of men of good will, which replaces a historic church based on revelation, which must be justified before the Tribunal of Reason. Kant tartly criticizes Herder's *Ideas on the Philosophy of History,* faulting him with two principal errors. First, Herder dissolved man in nature — ignoring that the moral enterprise is decidedly the work of freedom. Second, he introduced reason, a purely human faculty, through the medium of superior beings.[7]

A good case can be made that the most interesting, albeit not the most distinguished, of Hegel's predecessors was G. E. Lessing (1729-1781), whose *Education of the Human Race* recalls Abbot Joachim's medieval tapestry in a minor key, defleshed of its intense, quasi-mystical spiritual-

---

113. "La madurez intelectual de Europe es Hegel." Xavier Zubiri, *Naturaleza, Historia, Dios* (Madrid: Editoria Nacional, 1963), 225.

4. Cited in Friedrich Überweg, *History of Philosophy,* trans. George S. Morris (New York: Charles Scribner's Sons, 1873), 2:181.

5. Überweg, *History of Philosophy,* 186-87.

6. Frederick Copleston, S.J., *A History of Philosophy: Kant* (Garden City: Doubleday Image, 1964), 123-24.

7. Emile Bréhier, *Historia de a Filosofía,* trad. Demetrio Nuñez (Buenos Aires: Editorial Sudamericana, 1962), 3:207, 219.

ity. Lessing possessed a critical talent of no little acuity, as evidenced by his *Hamburg Dramaturgy*. A product of the Enlightenment, he contrasted the "voice of healthy reason" proper to his own age to those other ages when superstition was general, as well as to those nations (such as Spain and Bohemia) presently submerged in pious ignorance.[8] Miracles are restricted to the physical world. In the moral world things retain their natural course for the idiosyncratic reason that "the theatre is to be the school of the moral world."[9] As in Kant, here also the moral upstages the religious.

The Education of the Human Race is a secularized, abbreviated version of Joachim's dramatic portrait. Lessing did not reject the Christian religion outright but viewed it as a mere phase destined to be surpassed by the human spirit as it advances in its apprehension of truth. God, he insisted, allows truths of reason to be presented under the guise of revelations so as to disseminate them rapidly. As Bréhier indicates, Lessing's religion is one "which exceeds and absorbs revelation."[10] The advance of humanity takes place in three stages. In the first — *childhood* — immediate gratification is pursued and truths are presented under the form of images. The Old Testament is its appropriate text. During the second — *youth* — reason makes itself evident by means of deduction and combination. The prime motivation is concern for the future, prosperity, and honor. Its text is the New Testament. In the third — *maturity* — revealed verities are elevated into truths of reason. Even when other motives are absent, duty is followed. Its text is the "New Eternal Gospel," promised by the books of the "New Covenant."[11]

In this scheme education replaces revelation. Lessing praised the medieval Joachimites for maintaining "the same economy of the same God . . . the same plan for a common education of the human race." However, they erred in believing that their contemporaries had vaulted from child-

8. G. E. Lessing, *Hamburg Dramaturgy*, trans. Helen Zimmern (New York: Dover, 1962), 7-8.

9. Lessing, *Hamburg Dramaturgy*, 9.

10. Bréhier, *Historia*, 3:158.

11. G. E. Lessing, *The Education of the Human Race*, trans. Fred W. Robertson (London: Keegan, Paul, Trench, 1883); Überweg, *History of Philosophy*, 2:120-21.

hood into adults "worthy of the third age without proper preparation and enlightenment."[12] This task, one suspects, would be assumed by Lessing and his associates. Characteristic of the age, the son of God is accorded only a subordinate importance. Lessing added the novel addenda that the human path to unlimited truth requires . . . demands . . . an ever-renewed existence. This resembles, perhaps parodies, the Christian mystical teaching of St. John of the Cross: the infinite journey of the beatified soul to its ultimate center in God.

Fichte (1762-1814) and Schelling (1775-1854) followed in the wake of Lessing. The former's *Lectures on the Science of Politics* (1813) advanced the theory that history marks the progression from an original inequality to equality structured by the rational arrangement of social relations. Fichte foresaw a "new world" in which the thought of freedom would be manifested in the external world. The transition from inequality to equality, which is to say the entire course of history, would take place through the alchemy of a radical type of education modeled on the Pestalozzian system.[13]

In Lowith's opinion, Schelling's thirty-sixth lecture on the *Philosophy of Revelation* is the most profound and original attempt to establish philosophically the reign of the spirit.[14] Again we encounter a triadic structure. The three ages of history correspond to Peter, Paul, and John. Peter is the apostle of the Father, Paul of the Son, and John of the Holy Spirit, an age which leads to the "complete truth" of the future, the perfect religion of mankind.[15]

Schelling proposed another, more original, schema. The first age is that of *Fate*. This is a tragic period in which the blind ruling power destroys what is most elevated, which then passes into the collective memory as a golden age and becomes the object of fervid expectation. The second age is that of *Nature*. It was initiated by the expansion of the Roman Republic and introduced 'mechanical conformity' to law. Nations

12. Cited by Karl Lowith, *Meaning in History* (Chicago: Univ. of Chicago Press, 1949), 208f.

13. Überweg, *History of Philosophy*, 2:211-12.

14. Lowith, *Meaning in History*, 209.

15. Lowith, *Meaning in History*, 209.

begin to approach each other. The isolated disciplines of morality, law, the arts, and the sciences begin to merge. *Providence* is the third and last age. The past reveals itself as the adumbration of providence imperfectly revealed.[16]

At the source of these speculations lies a novel conception described in Schelling's "General Deduction of the Dynamic Process" (1800-1801). It depicts the progressive development of a gigantic mind. Immured within the confines of nature, this Leviathan surges into consciousness through the medium of humanity. Inspired by Giordano Bruno, he advocates a human autonomy that borders on self-deification. Man can contemplate the world and say, "I am the God whom it cherishes in its bosom, the mind that moves all things."[17] Hegel will further expand and embellish this scenario. It is not without importance that the original manifesto of German Idealism came from Hegel's pen, was drafted by Schelling and provided with poetic élan by Hölderlin. It celebrated the arrival of the "new man" and envisioned a synthesis of reason and myth that would elevate humanity to the third and highest stage of historical development.[18]

G. W. F. Hegel (1770-1831) has presented serious difficulties to philosophers, among the most notorious being Bertrand Russell. Hegel's thought is often viewed as a modern-day analogue to Hildegard von Bingen's *Lingua Ignota,* lacking a key to interpretation. However, in spite of twists and turns, additions and subtractions, convoluted argument and dense reasoning, a certain continuity can be discerned. His first work, the *Leben Jesu* (The Life of Jesus), was followed by other predominantly religious works that placed him squarely in the Enlightenment camp. He portrayed a Kantian Jesus who fulminates against positive religion (a religion based on authority) while preaching that morality is "the aim and essence of all true religion."[19]

As morality is grounded in freedom, Hegel castigates the "Jewish mentality" that he equates with the "otherworldly mentality." Abraham,

16. Überweg, *History of Philosophy,* 2:219-20.

17. Überweg, *History of Philosophy,* 2:219-20.

18. Frank E. Manuel, *Shapes of Philosophical History* (Stanford: Stanford Univ. Press, 1965), 120-21.

19. Hegel, *On Christianity,* trans. Knox and Kroner (New York: Harper, 1961), 68-69.

its representative, is chastised as a stranger to the earth, as is Abraham's God for making the "horrible claim" that he alone is God.[20] The confession of Peter (Matthew 16:13ff.) is interpreted as signifying the recognition of God in man. Man *(anthropos)* is the light *(phos)* that encounters its essence in God.[21]

The center of Hegel's thought is the notion of Absolute Spirit. It is the prime reality, undergirding both nature and spirit. Creation is the point of departure for the quest of Absolute Spirit to achieve its wholeness, its plenitude. Metaphysically speaking, history is not the succession of events that occur in time but is rather the essence of this succession . . . historicity.[22] The Absolute Spirit alienates, externalizes itself in nature, dividing itself into physical nature and finite spirit, only to overcome this alienation and return into itself as spirit. Philosophy is the discipline which studies this process of self-alienation, unfolding, and completion.

The process is dialectical. It advances from thesis — the abstract element of thought — to antithesis — nature — and culminates in synthesis — spirit.[23] Reduced to a temporal enclave, the dialectic functions when a civilization such as Greece (thesis) generates its opposite, Rome (antithesis), and out of thesis and antithesis produces a synthesis, the Christian world. The dialectical movement unites truth and reality by ascending from below to above, from exterior to interior, by means of a series of operations that suppress, preserve, and surpass, all of which are designated by the term *Aufheben.* As the dialectical movement of thought is identical to the dialectical movement of matter, Hegel bridges the Cartesian abyss between thought *(res cogitans)* and matter *(res extensa)* while providing a scaffolding for the philosophical comprehension of history.

Hegel was not exempt from the enthusiasm propagated by the Enlightenment. He was caught up in the maelstrom as were most others. The present is "a birth-time and a time of transition . . . the spirit of man has broken with the old order of things . . . let them all sink into the

20. Hegel, *On Christianity,* 186-88.

21. Hegel, *On Christianity,* 242; Matthew 16:13f.: "'And you,' he asked, 'who do you say I am?' Simon Peter answered: 'you are the Messiah, the Son of the living God'" (NEB).

22. Cf. Zubiri, *Naturaleza,* 229, 235-36.

23. Überweg, *History of Philosophy,* 2:231-32.

depths of the past and set about its own transformation."[24] The *Zeitgeist* (Spirit of the Times) advances slowly and quietly, at first appearing as a 'bare generality', like a new born child.[25]

The four great divisions of Hegel's philosophy are phenomenology, logic, natural philosophy, and philosophy of the spirit. History, together with psychology, law, and the science of customs, is included under philosophy of spirit. Historical fact deals with particular existences, with contingent and arbitrary events. While nature is spirit externalized, history is the process of its becoming in terms of knowledge. Hegel speaks of "a slow procession and succession of 'spiritual shapes' *(Geister)*, a gallery of pictures, each of which is endowed with the entire wealth of spirit."[26] This solemn progress takes place dialectically and advances towards the revelation of the depths of spiritual life that Hegel calls the Absolute Notion.

Hegel's clearest exposition of his thought on the subject is found in his *Lectures on the Philosophy of History.*[27] He again insists that the history of the world presents us with a rational process. Reason is the "substance" and "infinite energy" of the universe, the "infinite complex of things," the "true," the "Eternal" that reveals itself in the world.[28] History constitutes the itinerary of the World-Spirit. Anaxagoras (Nous governs the world) and the religious conception of providence — two highly unlikely bedfellows — are cited as presenting anticipations of his thought.

Hegel disagrees with the common belief that it is impossible to know God, which is attached to the religious notion of providence. On the contrary, the very fact that God has revealed himself to mankind renders such knowledge obligatory: "The thinking spirit . . . must advance to the intellectual comprehension of what was posited in the first instance to feeling and imagination."[29] This is to say that the content of religious belief must

---

24. Hegel, *The Phenomenology of Mind*, trans. J. P. Baillie (1910; London: Allen & Unwin, 1964), 75.

25. Hegel, *Phenomenology*, 80-81.

26. Hegel, *Phenomenology*, 807.

27. Hegel, *Lectures on the Philosophy of History*, trans. J. Sibree (New York: Dover, 1956).

28. Hegel, *Lectures*, 9-10.

29. Hegel, *Lectures*, 15.

be extracted from its imaginative husk and be appropriated by reason. When this is done it becomes evident that the history of the world is nothing but the progressive consciousness of the idea of *freedom*.[30]

History proceeds from East to West. It moves from the Eastern nations who knew that only one (the ruler) is free, to the Greek and Roman worlds in which some (the aristocrats) are free, culminating in German Christianity that knows that all (man as man) are free. These stages of the consciousness of freedom correspond to the 'natural division' of universal history. And the progressive consciousness of the idea of freedom is, *ipso facto,* the reality of freedom.[31] 'Freedom' in the language of reason is simply 'God's will' in the language of religion.

Hegel provides a catalogue of ships, an atlas of history beginning with Asia and culminating with Prussia. China, India, Persia (where "continuous history" begins), Assyria, Babylonia, and Phoenicia, lead up to the Hebrews.[32] The spiritual is encountered entirely purified and develops in opposition to nature. The idea of light, introduced in Persia by Zoroaster, advances to that of Yahweh, the "purely one." This marks the boundary between East and West.[33] However, Judaism is still flawed in that it is the family, and not the individual, which possesses inherent value, and this is reflected by its ignorance of immortality.

Hegel's land of heart's desire is Greece; we feel ourselves at home in the region of the spirit. Thought is revealed to be the inner being of nature and exists only in human consciousness.[34] It is a youthful protest against the age-encrusted East. Both Achilles, the ideal youth of poetry, and Alexander, the ideal youth of reality, were in radical opposition to Asia. In the shadow of Greece, Rome effects the transition "from the inner sanctum of subjectivity to its direct opposite."[35] Julius Caesar inaugurates the modern world while Augustus reveals its inner, spiritual existence.[36]

30. Hegel, *Lectures,* 456.
31. Hegel, *Lectures,* 19.
32. Hegel, *Lectures,* 99-188.
33. Hegel, *Lectures,* 195.
34. Hegel, *Lectures,* 220-23.
35. Hegel, *Lectures,* 281.
36. Hegel, *Lectures,* 318.

With Christianity we come upon a new principle, the *axis* on which the history of the world turns. Christ is the alpha and omega of history, its starting point as well as its goal as "the nature of God as pure Spirit is manifested to man."[37] Moreover, the 'real attestation' of Christ's divinity is not provided by miracles but rather by the witness of our own spirit. The Spirit's progress reaches its acme in the German spirit, which is the spirit of the "new world" and aims at the realization of absolute truth. The German peoples were destined to be the bearers of the Christian principle — absolute freedom.[38] The Reformation made the "principle of the Free Spirit" into the banner of a world striving toward the "world of completion," which will be attained at the end of days. The principle of thought, Hegel urges, "brings us to the last stage in history, our world, our own time."[39] Eschatology is made immanent. The End Time is now.

Two aspects of Hegel's thought merit further consideration: his attitude towards the German people and the Prussian State, which a critic might view as fawning, and his possible connection with esoteric currents of thought. Regarding the first, typical is Hegel's elocution of Oct. 22, 1818, in which the natural affinity between the Prussian State and his philosophy is celebrated.[40] Because of its affinity to the Christian spirit, the German race is the goal of the *Weltgeist* (World Spirit). It possesses those natural qualities that allow its members to receive the highest revelations of the Spirit. However, this is not, he insists, an affirmation of superiority as such, but refers only to the status of the German race during the final stage of history.[41] History reaches its apogee in the Prussian State.

Insofar as the influence of esoteric and "mystical" currents is concerned, the closest at hand were the "Suabian Fathers," and in particular, Oetinger (1702-1782). Although it is difficult to ascertain the extent of his influence, the Württemberg theologian advocated a view loosely resem-

37. Hegel, *Lectures,* 323.
38. Hegel, *Lectures,* 341f.
39. Hegel, *Lectures,* 442.
40. Cited in Jacques Chevalier, *Historia del Pensamiento,* trans. Jose Antonio Miguez (Madrid: Aguilar, 1963), 4:5-6.
41. Bréhier, *Historia,* 3:387.

bling that of Hegel: a progressive Divine revelation in which God goes out of himself only to return to himself, ultimately rising to the discovery of the trinitarian image.[42] But even if Oetinger's influence were negligible, there is little doubt that Hegel was attracted by esoteric speculation. Hölderlin indicated that when the "friends" said their farewells at Tubingen, their password was "the Kingdom of God."[43] Less than a year later, Hegel wrote to Schelling: "Come to us in the Kingdom of God. . . . Reason and Freedom remain our password and the invisible Church our meeting place."[44] Romantic fervor was combined with Teutonic pedantry.

At first sight Hegel's philosophy of history seems to obliterate the *Civitas Terrena*. All history is sacred. It is the stage on which the Spirit undergoes its exile and homecoming. The supporting cast is made up of those peoples who have formed states, the terrestrial aspects of the universal. The preeminence of a given state marks the triumph of a particular spiritual principle. History in its entirety is a manifestation of Spirit. However, by interpreting the Christian religion in terms of speculative reason Hegel did not obliterate the *Civitas Terrena* but melded the Kingdom of God to the history of mankind. He created a *Doppelgänger* of Augustine's *Civitas Dei,* completely earthbound, in which man is the Theotokos, the God-bearer, scarcely distinguishable, if at all, from the God he bears.

Hegel's early notion of God as mankind's handmaiden is not discarded but further elaborated. The Absolute Spirit is not the Christian God. The Absolute Religion is not traditional Christianity. The 'Kingdom of God' which surges through history is not Augustine's *Civitas Dei.* By eviscerating its dogmatic core Hegel succeeded in transforming Christianity, furthering a process begun by the Reformation. Is it only a happy coincidence that the *Phenomenology of Mind* was published in 1806, the same year that Goethe completed the first part of *Faust?*

Of the vast expanse of history, philosophy is primarily interested in the eternal present.[45] This is the center from which radiate the moving im-

---

42. Chevalier, *Historia,* 4:17.

43. Letter from Hölderin to Hegel (July 10, 1794). Cited in Chevalier, *Historia,* 4:19.

44. Letter from Hegel to Schelling (Jan. 1795). Cited in Chevalier, *Historia,* 4:19.

45. Cited in Bréhier, *Historia,* 3:384.

ages of temporal events governed by Hegel's notion of providence, "the concept of Reason . . . the sovereign of the world."[46] Insofar as the Christian notion of providence is concerned he dismisses it as a "peddler's view,"[47] as it fails to perceive the ultimate design. This "ultimate design" is safeguarded in Hegel's philosophy by means of his theory of the "cunning of reason," which implements the ultimate design in spite of the vagaries of human motivation. The final results of historical action are always more or less than that intended by its agents. Men are instruments of a power greater than themselves. Passions coalesce to form patterns of activity pliant to the dictates of Reason and alien to their immediate goals. The realization of right order is achieved surreptitiously and indirectly.

History is not simply the celestial music of the spheres liberated from all dissonance. On emerging from the Hegelian thought-box we find that history has become monolithically secular. It no longer includes, as in Vico, an authentic if embarrassing religious enclave. Small wonder, as Père de Lubac indicates, that Hegel opened the door to Feuerbach (Christianity as psychological illusion), Strauss (Christianity as historical illusion), and Marx (Christianity as eudaemonistic illusion).[48]

It was Hegel's notion of Objective Spirit that provided Comte with a device to structure the disparate and imprecise ideas of the French Physiocrats into the general lines and the vocabulary of sociology.[49] Years later Martin Heidegger identified the "living historical spirit" he had come to know in Hegel as the force that had made the "system of Catholicism" problematic and unacceptable.[50]

In spite of the objections which can be brought to bear against his system, Hegel remains a monumental figure in the history of philosophy, perhaps still more important in the philosophy of history. His systematic

46. Cited in Bréhier, *Historia,* 3:386.

47. Lowith, *Meaning in History,* 54-55.

48. Henri de Lubac, S.J., *The Dawn of Atheistic Humanism* (Cleveland: Meridian, 1963), 8f.

49. Xavier Zubiri, *Cinco Lecciones de Filosofía* (Madrid: Sociedad de Estudios y Publicaciones, 1963), 120.

50. Letter from Heidegger to Krebs (1918). Cited by Rüdiger Safranski, *Martin Heidegger: Between Good and Evil* (Cambridge: Harvard Univ. Press, 1998), 67.

talent, coupled with an almost lyric management of ideas, birthed an impressive and highly influential system of thought. In spite of his transmogrification of Christianity, Hegel retained elements of traditional Christianity that were not discarded until Marx succeeded in inverting the hierarchy of thought and activity, contemplation and work. As Hannah Arendt has indicated, the philosophies of Kierkegaard, Marx, and Nietzsche would not have been possible without the synthesizing achievement of Hegel and his concept of history.[51] Lowith was only slightly exaggerating when he credited Hegel with making German philosophy into world philosophy.[52]

51. Hannah Arendt, *Between Past and Future* (1961; New York: Penguin, 1993), 38.
52. Karl Lowith, *From Hegel to Nietzsche* (New York: Columbia Univ. Press, 1991), 308f.

CHAPTER 8

The Cult of Progress

S ir Isaiah Berlin was surely suffering from dyspepsia when he referred to "the knock-kneed army of eighteenth and nineteenth century philosophies of history."[1] Whether or not their work is to be admired (in spite of many flaws), their enthusiasm and optimism, in a period characterized by revolution and unsettlement, is surely extraordinary. The potent lure of an approaching paradise, of the reign of love, broadcast by the gospel of a new golden age, captures the sentiment of the time. It is found in Saint-Simon, Turgot, Condorcet, Comte, and others. The ineluctable march of Progress is also found in less ecstatic thinkers such as Adam Smith. The euphoria produced by the French Revolution and its aftermath issued into social change that was also furthered by the Physiocrats and the advances made by science: Newton's mechanics, chemistry, and the method in Fourier's analytic theory of heat.[2]

Beginning with the pragmatic aspect of this movement, we find Adam Smith (1723-1790) and his epoch-making *Wealth of Nations*. Primarily dedicated to moral theory, he attacked Mandeville because of the moral rigorism in his *Theory of Moral Sentiments* while condemning the insufficiency of intellectualistic ethics. However, he retained from Mandeville

1. Isaiah Berlin, *Russian Thinkers,* ed. H. Hardy and A. Kelly (New York: Penguin, 1981), 49.
2. Xavier Zubiri, *Cinco Lecciones de Filosofía* (Madrid: Sociedad de Estudios y Publicaciones, 1963), 119-21.

the notion of the perfect accord between natural egotism and social utility that provided the groundwork of his economic theory. The immediate sympathy or repulsion which Smith declared was the director of the moral life was not haphazard but followed the guidance of Providence. This signifies, in political economy, that the spontaneous play of egotism suffices — barring external interference — to augment the wealth of nations.

Harold Laski was not mistaken when he stated that "with Adam Smith, the practical maxims of business enterprise achieved the status of a theology."[3] Smith's principles are clear. The prime drive of man as an economic being is self-interest. There exists a natural order in the universe which guarantees that all individual strivings in favor of self-interest add up to the social good: the doctrine of laissez-faire. On the surface, the theory seems to be Hegel's "cunning of reason" applied to the realm of economics. The progressive state, as Adam Smith indicates, when society is advancing to further acquisition, rather than the static one, when it has acquired its full complement of riches, is the happiest and the most favorable to all orders of society.[4] Humanity progressively advances towards the Seven Cities of Gold.

Charles Fourier (1772-1837) is a good example of the romantic utopian spirit that finds its apogee in Auguste Comte. Gilson indicated that "the ghost of Rousseau is haunting the doctrine."[5] In *Le nouveau monde industriel et societaire* (1829-1830), Fourier captured the growing frenzy for the "new" by claiming to have made a great discovery. It certainly was unsettling: the principle that there exists a natural harmony between the different passions of the soul. This was interpreted to signify that personal and social happiness would prevail if the passions were unhindered and allowed to develop freely,[6] a variation of Rousseau and the revolutionary

---

3. Cited by Lerner in his introduction to Adam Smith, *An Enquiry into the Nature and Causes of the Wealth of Nations,* edited by Edwin Cannon and Max Lerner (New York: Modern Library, 1937), ix.

4. Smith, *Wealth of Nations,* 81.

5. Etienne Gilson, Thomas Langan, and Armand Maurier, *Recent Philosophy: Hegel to the Present* (New York: Random House, 1962), 751n.1.

6. Gilson, Langan, and Maurier, *Recent Philosophy,* 751n.1.

maxim: do away with limitations and all will be well. Man is not a dangerous animal to be kept in chains but a near-deity whose impulses are sacrosanct.

Fourier's vision, utopian and revolutionary, was catapulted into the practical order. Communities following his inspiration were founded. Although the only phalanstery (community) set up in France during his lifetime was a failure, they burgeoned in the United States where Albert Brisbane (1809-1890) popularized his thought. Between 1840 and 1850 at least forty-one American phalansteries were founded. Analogous communities were established by Etienne Cabet (1788-1856), a disciple of Robert Owen, who, influenced by More's *Utopia,* founded a colony at St. Louis, Missouri, where he died.

However, it was Antoine-Nicolas de Condorcet (1743-1794) who led the way in framing a philosophy of history from the viewpoint of progress. Something of a child prodigy, he was educated by the Jesuits at the College de Navarre. At twenty-two years of age he submitted his *Essai sur le calcul intégral* to the Academie des Sciences, where it earned plaudits from Lagrange and D'Alembert. He later joined the circle around Voltaire and the great *Encyclopaedia.* A disciple and friend of Turgot, Condorcet was deeply influenced by his addresses before the Sorbonne on the progressions of the human mind. They acted as the point of departure for his influential *Sketch (Esquisse d'un Tableau des progrès de l'esprit Humain),* which has been called the canonical French text on the idea of progress.[7] Emulating the method of the eighteenth-century church historians, Condorcet applied it in a deliberately anticlerical spirit.[8]

It is one of the many ironies of history that Condorcet was able to compose, in an age of upset and in the very shadow of the guillotine,[9] a

7. Frank E. Manuel, *Shapes of Philosophical History* (Stanford: Stanford Univ. Press, 1965), 96-97.

8. R. G. Collingwood, *The Idea of History* (New York: Oxford Univ. Press, 1956), 80-81.

9. In June 1793, he was a member of the Committee of Public Safety, together with Robespierre. He voted against the execution of the king and went into hiding after attacking the new Jacobin constitution. Identified as an aristocrat, Condorcet was arrested and imprisoned. The following day he was found dead in his cell, possibly a suicide.

work tracing human progress from superstition and barbarism to enlightenment. His originality consisted in extending the doctrine of progress to every department of human activity, viewing them as interconnected. This follows from his theory of knowledge, grounded in sensism. The first sentence of the *Sketch* provides the scaffolding: "Man is born with the ability to receive sensations."[10]

History is an uninterrupted chain linking the beginning of historical time and the century in which Condorcet lived.[11] In spite of provisional setbacks, humanity lumbers forward. Cosmic disaster to one side, humanity can be assured of continuous progress in enlightenment, freedom, and equality. Condorcet divides the history of mankind into ten stages or eras: (1) Men uniting into tribes; (2) the pastoral and agricultural peoples; (3) the invention of the alphabet; (4) the Greek mind up to the division of the sciences; (5) the decline of the sciences; (6) the renewal of the sciences at the time of the Crusades; (7) the early progress of science; (8) philosophy and the sciences shaking off the yoke of authority; (9) Descartes to the foundation of the French Republic.[12]

Insofar as the tenth and last stage is concerned, dealing with the future progress of the human mind, Condorcet asks:

> If man can . . . predict phenomena when he knows their laws . . . (and can) . . . forecast the future on the basis of his experience of the past, why, then, should it be regarded as a fantastic undertaking to sketch with some pretense of truth, the future destiny of man on the basis of his history?[13]

He fully expected the future to be superior to the present and looked forward to the abolition of inequality: between nations, within nations, be-

---

10. Antoine-Nicholas de Condorcet, *Sketch for a Historical Picture of the Progress of the Human Mind,* trans. June Barraclough (Westport: Greenwood Press, 1979), 3.

11. Condorcet, *Sketch,* 8.

12. Condorcet, *Sketch.* Stage 1, 14-18; stage 2, 19-24; stage 3, 25-40; stage 4, 41-54; stage 5, 55-76; stage 6, 77-88; stage 7, 89-98; stage 8, 99-123; stage 9, 124-172; stage 10, 173-202.

13. Condorcet, *Sketch,* 173.

tween peoples, all leading to the true perfection of mankind. The time will come "when the sun will shine only on free men who know no other master than their reason."[14]

Equality and reason are the principal terms. If inequality in wealth, status, and education diminished notably, real equality would be attained. Condorcet did not harbor plans of radically altering human nature but believed that man's instruments — the prostheses of his intelligence — would increase and improve. This would augment the force and speed of his mind.[15] It would allow mankind to move towards equality between the sexes, abolish customs dictated by prejudice, and contemplate the formulation of a meta-language, or even the prospect of prolonging human life . . . perhaps indefinitely. Most important, Condorcet maintained that those causes that contribute to the perfection of the human race must, by their very nature, exercise a *perpetual influence* and constantly increase their sphere of activity.[16] An unstoppable, accelerating march to Utopia.

God is eliminated. Nature is reduced to an élan promising indefinite progress, while lacking a determinate goal or end. Stuart Hampshire has indicated that "Condorcet saw the outlines of liberal democracy more than a century in advance of his time."[17] Though somewhat of an exaggeration, his opinion can be accepted with only minor reservations. In any case, Condorcet, in spite of being carried along on the tidal wave of utopianism, was not blind to the dangers of his ideology. Inequality should diminish but not disappear. It is the result of natural and necessary causes and if it in fact should disappear, this would introduce additional sources of inequality and imperil the rights of man.[18] It will remain for Auguste Comte, a more complex, pathological, but philosophically gifted personality, to develop — transmute might be a better term — elements encountered in Condorcet's thought into an influential philosophy of history.

A few words about Count Claude-Henri de Saint-Simon (1760-1825) would be advisable before passing on to Comte. He was the dominant in-

14. Condorcet, *Sketch*, 179.
15. Condorcet, *Sketch*, 185.
16. Condorcet, *Sketch*, 193f., 199.
17. Condorcet, *Sketch*, Intro., p. x.
18. Condorcet, *Sketch*, 179-80.

tellectual personality of the Age because of his verve, exuberant fantasy, and visionary afflatus. A checkered career: government official, business failure, pamphlet writer; a man who fought on the American side in the War of Independence, participated in the French Revolution, and who was imprisoned during the Terror.[19] His *New Christianity (Le nouveau christianisme, dialogue entre un conservateur et un novateur,* 1825) marked the epoch and exercised a great influence.

In Saint-Simon's opinion, the "New Christianity" is not radically different from the old as the "permanent base" of Christianity remains the same: the moral rule to love one another. The traditional Christian religions have lost their sense of mission and no longer respond to social needs. Catholicism is the bulwark of reaction. Protestantism subordinates religion to the state.[20] The role of the New Christianity is to reorganize society by giving new force to the evangelical precept of love. To accomplish this Saint-Simon would replace saints with philanthropists, clergy with scientists, nobility with bankers, and ambassadors with captains of industry.

Several points of departure for a future philosophy of history are found in Saint-Simon. First, that in the sciences there is a necessary advance from conjectural state to the positive, an idea he had garnered from a Dr. Berdin in 1798. He pointed to the "science of man" (which in 1814, he placed in Positive Politics) as one that has yet to reach the positive state. Second, he characterized his own era as one of transition, placed between the destruction of the old system and the establishment of the new.[21] Third, he defined religion as a system of ideas by which the sages of an epoch represent the universe. As every religion expresses the science of its Age, it follows that as scientific ideas change so do the religious: "The science of today is the religion of yesterday."[22]

In his *Système industriel* (1821), Saint-Simon maintains that the conditions for lasting peace will be provided by a coalition of industrial inter-

19. Gilson, Langan, and Maurier, *Recent Philosophy,* 752n.3; Emile Bréhier, *Historia de a Filosofía,* trad. Demetrio Nuñez (Buenos Aires: Editorial Sudamericana, 1962), 3:447f.

20. Bréhier, *Historia,* 3:449-50.

21. Bréhier, *Historia,* 3:447-49.

22. Henri Gouhier, *La Vie d'Auguste Comte* (Paris: Librarie Gallkimard, 1931), 18, 20.

ests. This augurs a coming renewal of society of which he would act as the Messiah. His followers further elaborated his speculations, larded as they are with fantasy. Many considered his doctrine to be the long-awaited revelation. A religion without asceticism was most appealing to the Age. Its adepts, which included Comte, Rodrigues, Bazard, and Enfantin, published in 1828 an authoritative text, *Exposition de la Doctrine*. Bréhier has nicely described it as "a strange mixture of subversive propaganda, naturalist morality, and the practical spirit of enterprise."[23] This would take root in the grotto-like mind of Comte to produce an abundant harvest of speculation of which the philosophy of history is the core.

Isidore Auguste Marie François Xavier Comte (1798-1857) was born in the sixth year of the Republic. His parents were fervent Catholics and discreet monarchists. An *enfant terrible*, he revolted against all authority while harboring a romanticized notion of the United States, *"terre sainte, refuge de la liberté, patrie de tous les republicains du monde."*[24] From the time that he acted as Saint-Simon's secretary, Comte was captivated by the idea that his was a transitional age, that a new age was beginning, an age in which the supernatural would give way to the earthly, the poetic to the real, and the conjectural to the positive. Moreover, he affirmed that once the philosophy of each individual science was established, the elements which are common to all would be discovered, and in this manner the "general philosophy of all the sciences" would be ascertained.[25]

Comte distanced himself from Saint-Simon shortly after he left his service. Saint-Simon died on May 19, 1825, believing that Comte, "Lucifer unmasked," had betrayed him. By 1829 Comte was referring to Saint-Simonism as "that warmed over theo-philanthropy" *(cette theophilanthropie réchauffée).*[26] After a period of mental derangement and personal anguish,[27] Comte was able to fulfill, in his own fashion, his mentor's am-

---

23. Bréhier, *Historia,* 3:452-53.

24. Gouhier, *Vie,* 42, 46.

25. Gouhier, *Vie,* 89, 111.

26. Letter to Gustave d'Eichthal (December 11, 1829). Gouhier, *Vie,* 13.

27. He married a prostitute, was treated for "mania" lapsing into a quasi-vegetative state, attempted suicide, recovered somewhat, but states of extreme irritability perdured along with other manifestations of psychopathology.

bition to establish a new spiritual authority and to structure a lasting philosophy of history.

A further, more bizarre, area of his thought was opened when he met Clotilde de Vaux, with whom he fell passionately in love, a love burdened with all the attributes of psychopathology. When she died, Comte raised her to celestial honors. The encounter inflamed his imagination to the point that he could state "religious positivism began in reality . . . May 16, 1845, when my heart proclaimed unexpectedly . . . one cannot always think but we can always love. . . ."[28] As early as 1847 Comte preached the advent of the "final religion" — the Religion of Humanity. By the spring of 1849 he declared that the new universal church had been instituted. In October of that year he began the introduction to his *Système de Politique Positive*. The system required the perfection of Clotilde. As she is the perfect type of humanity his love for her and man's love for humanity is directed towards the same goal. This is to say that Comte loves humanity by means of Clotilde.[29] He is hailed as *"le Grand Prêtre de L'Humanité."*

Comte's ever present aspiration, inherited from Saint-Simon, of substituting humanity for the "divine phantom" of established Christianity, had been fulfilled. The means of accomplishing the task had been discovered. It was a science. Its name is sociology, a term first used by Comte with regard to the work of Condorcet.[30] Towards the end of his life, the Religion of Humanity attempted to evangelize, sending "missionaries" to England, Holland, Spain, and even the United States. When he died the sacred formula of Positivism was inscribed on his tomb: "Love and Progress."[31]

Comte's philosophy of history dates from his very first opuscules and is probably the oldest part of his thought. He drew up a plan, in 1822, outlining the projected work. It has three sections, beginning with historical data concerning the march of the human spirit, passing to Positive Education, and ending with the action of man over nature.[32] He was prodded

28. Gouhier, *Vie,* 267.

29. Gouhier, *Vie,* 259, 274, 277.

30. Gouhier, *Vie,* 258; Karl Lowith, *Meaning in History* (Chicago: Univ. of Chicago Press, 1949), 72; 233n.31.

31. Gouhier, *Vie,* 288.

32. Bréhier, *Historia,* 3:474.

in this direction by the vicissitudes of the postrevolutionary period, especially the disintegration of the spiritual power of the church. He was convinced that the chaotic state of affairs reached to only one form of society. Society itself cannot be destroyed. There is no critical epoch but rather a historical movement, an organic growth, in which one epoch is extinguished while another epoch is being prepared. There is a general law regarding the development of the human mind that is also applicable to the individual sciences.

This is the Law of the Three States.

The human mind — and each branch of knowledge — passes successively through three states or stages. It begins with the *Theological,* is followed by a transitional stage, the *Metaphysical,* and culminates in the *Positive* or *Scientific,* its ultimate, fixed, goal. Each stage corresponds to a different mode of philosophy and pertains to a different class. In the Theological, pertaining to the aristocracy, the mind aims at knowing the intimate nature of being, at absolute knowledge, and appeals to supernatural agents. These supernatural agents are replaced by abstract forces, inherent in the various types of beings, in the Metaphysical stage, proper to the bourgeoisie. Finally, the Positive, which is proper to all classes, although the proletariat (as *tabula rasa*) is the best positioned to accept it, aims at discovering the laws which govern the succession and similarity of phenomena.[33]

Each stage has an acme. The first stage reaches its perfection when it concludes there is one God, the second when it attains the general idea of Nature, while the third tends irresistibly, but without assurance of success, to place all phenomena under a single law. In the shadow of medieval genetics and adumbrating Freud's psychoanalytic theory, Comte realized that the individual is an abbreviated recapitulation of the development of the entire species. The three stages are also illustrated in the life of the individual. Man is a theologian in childhood, a metaphysician in his youth, and a physicist in his maturity.

The plot of history is of the essence. As Comte states in his *Cours de Philosophie Positive:* "To explain the true nature and proper character of

33. Zubiri, *Cinco Lecciones,* 136, 150, 160-61.

positive philosophy, it is necessary to survey as a whole the progress of the human spirit, for a concept is understood only through its history."[34] His aspiration to construct an encyclopedic ladder of the fundamental sciences was implemented. Beginning with astronomy, physics, chemistry, physiology, and social physics, he later added sociology, and, in his *Système,* contemplated another science, superior to sociology, which he called morality. This is required by the prominent role played by sentiment, the ultimate source of the cult of humanity. From this perspective, the different sciences are branches of morality.[35] This bears out John Stuart Mill's observation that Comte was a morality-intoxicated man.[36]

The study of social phenomena, according to Comte, had languished in a deplorable state of paralyzed infantilism. A new science was required so as to curb the menacing chaos of the interim period. To do this it was imperative to reconcile order and progress in spite of their present cleavage as their conjunction comprises the principal strength of any political system.[37] This, he believed, was possible in France. Only one thing was required, "a political doctrine of sufficient rationality to be always, in action, consistent with its own principles."[38]

The method of Positive Philosophy is summarized in two notions: the idea of continuous progress, and the search for the laws of continuity, as it is continuity that determines the direction of human development.[39] The human condition possesses a "spontaneous" and "irresistible" tendency towards improvement that is continuous, "a gradual amelioration within the proper limits."[40] Comte makes an interesting proviso. Historical speculation should be kept within the limits of the elite of European nations (France, England, Germany, Spain, and Italy). Each will progress accord-

34. *The Essential Comte* (selected from the *Cours de Philosophie Positive*), ed. Stanislau Andreski, trans. Margaret Clarke (London: Croom Helm, 1974), 19.

35. Bréhier, *Historie,* 4:187.

36. John Stuart Mill, *Auguste Comte and Positivism* (Ann Arbor: Univ. of Michigan Press, 1961), 139-40, 141, 176.

37. *Essential Comte,* 125-27.

38. *Essential Comte,* 127, 130.

39. *Essential Comte,* 162-63.

40. *Essential Comte,* 169.

ing to its own proper genius. To include other nations would be the source of monumental confusion.[41] Like Vico and Hegel the upward course of history is limited to the Occidental nations.

The Positive Era began with Bacon, Galileo, and Descartes, whose *Discourse on Method* should be extended and completed by means of the historico-sociological method which will make the philosophy of history scientific.[42] This, Comte suggests, could lead humanity to a universal regime characterized by harmony and free common development. The present industrial regime, in which *techne* has acquired a social character, is grist for Positivism's mill, and complements the march of progress, which consists in the ever stronger affirmation of humanity over animality.

To complement his program, *"Reorganiser, sans Dieu ni roi, par le culte systématique de l'humanité,"* Comte needed a social mucilage to bind men together. This was the role of his 'Religion of Humanity', a fanciful, rather bizarre concoction, with strong links to the unconscious. He borrowed from Catholicism, contending that although its doctrine was otiose, its organization was not and could be reconstituted on a secular basis. J. S. Mill, although he catalogued many of its odd and grotesque particulars,[43] realized that behind the ridiculous facade lay a serious aspiration: "the necessity of a Spiritual Power, distinct and separate from the temporal government."[44] In 1851, M. Comte predicted that before 1860 he would preach the Gospel of Positivism in the Cathedral of Notre Dame.

Positivism cut a large swath in European intellectuality and society. It worked powerfully in the minds of men, especially in the French and English, inspiring thinkers of stature such as Bentham, the Mills, and Littre. Even when many detached themselves from Comte because of the exaggerations of the Religion of Humanity, they acknowledged his elevation

---

41. *Essential Comte,* 199-200; 232-33.

42. Lowith, *Meaning in History,* 69.

43. The *"Vrais anges gardiens"* are mother, wife, and daughter; a method of prayer patterned after St. Ignatius's *Exercises* (two hours a day); a public cultus with 84 festivals, nine sacraments, Paris as the religious capital of the world, and the hope of 'subjective immortality', i.e., living in the memory of mankind. Mill, *Auguste Comte,* 150-52; 167-68.

44. Mill, *Auguste Comte,* 153, 155.

of the idea of humanity to new heights. J. S. Mill noted that Comte was among the few who had realized the majesty of which the idea of humanity is capable,[45] and believed him a thinker of the same category as Descartes and Leibniz!

Auguste Comte was a strange blend of scientific rigor, unbridled romanticism, and utopian vision, all embroidered with psychopathology. The importance of his philosophy of history — a secular analogue to that of Joachim of Fiore — was immense, perhaps because of its unique character. The Law of the Three Stages marked a watershed, to be followed, reacted against, imitated, and plundered. In its de-intellectualized popular version, Comte's doctrine settled comfortably in the mass imagination to become a pillar of public orthodoxy. Even today, after over a century and a half of disillusionment with scientism and the panaceas of the nineteenth century, much of Comte's program is still pullulating beneath the surface of contemporary society.

45. Mill, *Auguste Comte,* 133, 137.

CHAPTER 9

Disillusion and History:
Traditionalism and the Pessimistic Vision

The optimism which birthed and to some extent followed the French Revolution, reflected in the theories of progress framed by Turgot, Condorcet, Saint-Simon, and others, was not shared by the adherents of the ancien régime. They believed that the philosopher's dream of a glorious humanity advancing to utopian heights was a noxious illusion, marking a plunge into the depths. Reason was held suspect as proceeding from the muddied waters of the *philosophes*. Irrationalism, as it defied explanation and could not be undermined by criticism, was made common cause with the recrudescence of Roman Catholicism. The Traditionalists were very much aware that the Revolution had been as much or more religious as it had been political.

The church had suffered. Events tilted to the catastrophic. Public worship was proscribed from 1792 to 1795. A great number of priests were in prison or in exile. Even later, for three years after the 1830 disturbances, priests did not dare to appear on the street in clerical garb. Herder proclaimed that "the Church of Rome is now but an ancient ruin, into which henceforth no new life can come."[1] The secularized and degraded versions of the "New Heaven" and the "New Earth" appeared to have superceded their scriptural originals.

1. Cited in Walter Marshall Horton, *The Philosophy of the Abbe Bautain* (New York: New York Univ. Press, 1926), 37.

Joseph Marie Comte de Maistre (1753-1821) and Vicomte Louis de Bonald (1754-1840) give the impression of being joined at the hip. As Maistre wrote Bonald: "I have thought nothing that you have not written; I have written nothing that you have not thought."[2] Ironically, although they frequently corresponded, the two men never met. Yet the similarity of their thought, indeed of their lives, is remarkable. They were both minor aristocrats, sincerely religious, casualties of the Revolution and exiles, and both surfaced to prominence with the Restoration. Both reacted vigorously against liberal optimism, its belief in the fundamental goodness of man, desiccated reason, and the inevitability of progress. They stressed the negative effects of original sin and advocated authority and repression to uphold civilization. They turned from the speculative to the organic, that chain forged by the links between the dead, the living, the as yet unborn, and the land on which they live.

Unfortunately, the Traditionalists were ignorant of their own tradition to a surprising degree. A good example of this is provided by a textbook, in five volumes, published in Lyon in 1792, and imposed by the Catholic hierarchy, the *Philosophia Lugdunensis.* Although published anonymously, it was the work of an Oratorian, Father Joseph Valla.[3] It enjoyed remarkable success. Yet its content was an eclectic melange of Aristotelianism, Cartesianism, and ontology, a bizarre mixture to merit the approval of the church authorities. More on target, Barbey d'Aurevilly included Bonald and Maistre, together with Chateaubriand and Lamennais, in his *The Prophets of the Past.*[4]

Bonald maintained that the Revolution was the most decisive of all events, that because of its depredations his was the first generation to be able to grasp the "whole movement" of history.[5] The Revolution was a *'novum,'* a horrifying upset, reserved for the "final instruction" of man-

2. Cited by Mary Hall Quinlan, *The Historical Thought of the Vicomte de Bonald* (Washington: Catholic University Press, 1953), 11.

3. Etienne Gilson, Thomas Langan, and Armand Maurier, *Recent Philosophy: Hegel to the Present* (New York: Random House, 1962), 713n.1.

4. Jacques Chevalier, *Historia del Pensamiento,* trans. Jose Antonio Miguez (Madrid: Aguilar, 1963), 4:262n.37.

5. Quinlan, *Historical Thought,* 48.

kind. It must have been extremely difficult for Bonald and his like to come to terms with the revolutionary vicissitudes: France descending from the most concentrated unity of power to the most abject demagoguery; from the most perfect religious constitution to the most infamous idolatry.[6] Or so he interpreted the event.

Bonald believed he represented "Catholic philosophy" when he set up revelation and authority against individual reason and private interpretation. Following Malebranche, he developed his notions of reason, nature, and law grounded on the nature of things. Attaching himself to the theory of 'primitive revelation', he taught that knowledge and certitude were based on a revelation made by God to man. Bonald accorded special importance to the gift of language, the point of departure of both thought and society. This develops through history to ultimately take the form of Christendom, "a gathering in a confederation of the more powerful and enlightened nations which ever existed."[7] Language, thought, and society all issue out of God's creative *fiat*.

What Bonald called 'sentiment', and which can be loosely translated as 'feeling' or 'impression', deals with existences, while thought deals only with the possible. It follows that God's existence is established through 'sentiment'. As all men, he urges, possess the *sentiment de Dieu* and as God is the source of language, it follows that Scripture, the language of God, is of the utmost importance to insure the preservation of society. But it does not follow that truth is static. Bonald admits a type of advance within the truth, a process by which ancient belief can develop in such a way as to become even more 'august' and 'lovable'.[8]

Society is not then established by contract, as a contract requires the existence of a society, however primitive. Society must predate the contract. For Bonald the primitive fact is power and *omnis potestas a Deo est* (Romans 13:1-2). Men are created alike but unequal. They enter into a system of relations between stronger and weaker which constitutes society. Society requires a unity of power which can be guaranteed by reli-

---

6. Bonald, *Législation primitive, Oeuvres,* I, 202-3.

7. Bonald, *Demonstration philosophique,* intro. Cited in Gilson, Langan, and Maurier, *Recent Philosophy,* 716n.5.

8. Bonald, *Demonstration philosophique,* intro.

gion. This is the basis of all societies: "The state must obey religion and, in turn, the ministers of religion have a duty to obey the state in all those of its prescriptions that agree with the laws of religion."[9]

A distinction essential to his philosophy of history is that between the *native* and the *natural* state. Bonald gives the acorn and child as examples of the native state; the full-grown tree and the adult as examples of the natural state. In religious and secular societies the native state pertains to their genesis, the natural to their perpetuation and conservation.[10] The native state of man is domestic society, which is perfected and consolidated in the natural state. Every society is made up of three 'social persons': Power, Minister, and Subject. In domestic society this translates into father, mother, and child; in religious society to God, priests, and the faithful; in political society to king, nobility, and subjects.[11]

His first work, *Théorie du pouvoir politique et religieux,* was confiscated by the Directory but came to the attention of Napoleon, who offered to have it reprinted. Later, he sounded out Bonald regarding a tract dealing with the freedom of the seas. Bonald, a staunch legitimist, refused.[12] The Restoration brought honors and opportunities to broadcast his thought. His last major work was a concise restatement of his views concerning the nature of society: *Démonstration philosophique du principe constitutif de la Société* (1827).

Although Bonald did not open new horizons in the philosophy of history he did add a novel twist by combining three theories into a single schema. The first, by now rather moth-eaten, is the analogy of history and the stages of human life. The second is that which Bonald calls "the law of the three stages," to wit: (1) the era of personal rule; (2) the era of public rule; (3) the era of popular rule. The third theory is based on the distinction between the native and the natural state, that is to say, the transition of society from primitivism to perfected civilization. Quinlan observes that "taken together they form a framework within which one

---

9. Gilson, Langan, and Maurier, *Recent Philosophy,* 213.
10. Gilson, Langan, and Maurier, *Recent Philosophy,* 212.
11. Gilson, Langan, and Maurier, *Recent Philosophy,* 212.
12. Quinlan, *Historical Thought,* 5-7.

may arrive at an understanding of Bonald's concept of development in history."[13] His thought is nicely articulated in the *Législation primitive*.[14]

The second, the law of the three stages, includes the other theories: "The three stages of power (personal, public, and popular) take into account all the accidental modifications of society: they include all the periods of power: its birth, its life, and its death."[15] When power is personal it generates fear as it is arbitrary, capricious, and violent. When public, it is buttressed by institutions and established relations based on law. When popular, it converts the king into a functionary of the sovereign people, and power ineluctably falls into the hands of the masses.

Bonald affirmed that when a chaotic era arises — one thinks of the interim between the Directorate and the Restoration — a strong leader can arise to reorganize society. In 1827, he cast Napoleon in this role. But Napoleon, a man who might have set in motion a new cycle of history, failed to construct anything durable in the political and religious domains. This is reflected in his failure to build either a palace or a church. None the less, Napoleon did initiate, albeit fitfully, the rehabilitation of the church. The Concordat of 1801 made Roman Catholicism the official religion of France, and the amnesty of 1802 brought back forty thousand emigrant nobles. The result was not encouraging. The church became an organ of the state, and priests its apologists and purveyors of useful information.

---

13. Quinlan, *Historical Thought,* 14.

14. "Society has, like the individual, its childhood, its adolescence, and its manhood. . . . Man is born imperfect, with an intellect undirected by will . . . political society begins in a state of ignorance regarding laws and weakness regarding action.

"Man becomes corrupted and passes into a stage where he has will power without reason . . . the stage of the 'robust child' as Hobbes calls it. Society becomes corrupted and passes into the state of error and passion characteristic of pagan peoples . . . people without reason in the midst of the splendor of their conquests.

"Man perfects himself and attains to his natural state, to the state of resonableness in will and virtue in action. Society becomes civilized and attains to its natural state, to wisdom in its laws, and strength and virtue in its institutions . . . one which has constituted, at least up to our days, the society of the Christian peoples." *Législation primitive, Oeuvres,* I, 333.

15. Cited in Quinlan, *Historical Thought,* 36f.

The Catholic reaction did not assume major proportions until the period between 1830 and 1848.

There is the presence of Vico as well as more than a trace of Enlightenment optimism in Bonald's thought. He agreed with Condorcet regarding the progressive enlightenment of the human race but contended that it would not be brought about by scientific advancement but rather by a deepening of the moral sense.[16] Morality is objective. Rational speculation is vitiated at its source. He faulted the rationalism of his day as the inevitable consequence of Descartes' attempt to philosophize *dans un poêle,* as a mind isolated from society and tradition.[17] However, as Maine de Biran noted, this pointed to a flaw in Bonald's thought, his blindness regarding interiority, the primitive fact of consciousness, the avenue by which God is heard in the depths of the soul.[18] Nevertheless, Bonald maintained a view at odds with the pedantic vagaries of the critical mind, a view that can be called organic. Comte believed that Bonald was the model of this type of thought.

Joseph de Maistre had a checkered career. He sat twenty years in a Gallican parliament and was a practicing Mason for sixteen, as he was persuaded that Masonry was the key to the union of the Christian churches. Impressed by Burke's *Reflections on the Revolution in France,* when the French invaded Savoy in September, 1792, he emigrated to Lausanne. He wrote *Lettres d'un royaliste savoisien* to inaugurate his literary career, which was established in 1797 with *Considérations sur la France.* The year marked a watershed in his life. Maistre veered in religion from Gallicanism to Ultramontanism; in politics from the views of a parochial Savoyard to that of a cosmopolitan European; in social thought, he discarded his illuminism as "mere silliness" and turned to orthodox Catholicism. His mission was to reconstitute Christianity on the authority of the Pope rid of fetters.[19]

Maistre settled in Saint Petersburg as Piedmontese ambassador to the Russian court, a post he held for sixteen years. His ties with the Jesuit com-

16. Quinlan, *Historical Thought,* 106.
17. Chevalier, *Historia,* 4:267-68.
18. Horton, *Philosophy of the Abbe,* 255.
19. René Johannet, *Joseph de Maistre* (Paris: Flammarion, 1932), 90, 128.

munity in St. Petersburg, an order proscribed in most European countries, led to his being removed from this post. His years in Russia matured his literary style, which can alternately soothe and caress — as when describing an evening boating on the Neva; or slash and cut — as when describing the virtues of the executioner. A keen but unsystematic thinker, Maistre often verged on the mystagogic, less often on the traditionally spiritual.[20]

Yet, he was usually clear and to the point, often nearly telegraphic, as when he speaks of the Pope:

> No public morals or national character without religion, no European religion without Christianity, no true Christianity without Catholicism, no Catholicism without the pope, no pope without the supremacy which belongs to him.[21]

Like Bonald, Maistre emphasized the importance of religion, a commodity, he suggests, of which Frenchmen stand in need. Lacking religion, they are mutilated, much to the joy of the Revolution, which, as a satanic upheaval, can only be corrected by a contrary principle. The papacy is the cornerstone of the contrary principle, religion its vital élan, the church its presence in space and time. Infallibility in the spiritual order and sovereignty in the temporal order are synonymous. Both express the higher power which dominates them.

Maistre, like Bonald, gave much thought to the role of language. He studied its vagaries and urged that any language subject to variation was unsuitable for the Christian cultus. The corruption of the world daily takes possession of certain words, deforming and spoiling them. Because of this, it would be possible for "any libertine" to render the sacred liturgy "ridiculous" and "indecent." Therefore, it is imperative that the language of religion should be kept free from the control of men.[22] Man is not com-

---

20. Johannet, *Joseph*, 16ff. Maistre speaks of "a certain inexpressible light which carries me off in spite of myself," of losing himself in the clouds . . . of his fascination for mystery, the arcane and Kabbalah (25, 32-33).

21. Letter of May 22, 1814. Cited by R. A. Lebrun in his introduction to *The Pope*, trans. Aeneas McD. Dawson (New York: Howard Fertig, 1975), xi.

22. Joseph de Maistre, *Du Pape* (Genève: Librarie Droz, 1966), 128.

pletely perverse. But as a paradoxical mixture of the perverse and the moral, he requires a sovereign, a strong hand.

Maistre was catholic in his dislikes. He castigated the clergy for cooperating, albeit unwillingly, in their own demise, noting as the first symptoms of decay their simultaneous loss of the power and the will to convert mankind.[23] More stridently, he attacked Locke's *Essay on Human Understanding* as the source of the current *theophobia,*[24] countering Locke's 'sensism' with his own version of Traditionalism. God originally granted man elevated power of intuition, but this has almost been lost. Proceeding from this conviction Maistre took up the cudgels in favor of instinct and innate ideas, of intuition over discursive reason. Even in science, discoveries are made by sudden flashes of insight while morality itself is grounded on the instincts of the race embodied in tradition and custom.[25]

These speculations lead to certain conclusions in the philosophy of history. Instead of an uninterrupted advance from barbarism to high civilization, Maistre posited an initial flash of illumination which progressively diminishes in intensity. Humanity is retrogressing not advancing. It unlearned what it first knew, and is engaged in the laborious task of recouping a portion of the loss. This advance, however limited, is the product of human effort, which will strain towards but never achieve the level of the original charism. However, there are hints in *Les soirées de Saint-Petersbourg* that he envisioned the coming of a new era in which science would redirect humanity from matter to spirit so that spirit could regain its primacy.[26]

A good argument can be made that Maistre was endeavoring to discover a bedrock which would authenticate historical development while restricting it within appropriate limits. This is evidenced by his theory of constitutions, put forward in *Considérations sur la France,* a work whose ripples reached the shores of the New World. The constitution is the work of God, a confluence of custom, tradition, and usage under the direction

23. Maistre, *Du Pape,* 320.

24. Joseph de Maistre, *St. Petersburg Dialogues,* trans. Richard A. Lebrun (Montreal: McGill-Queens University Press, 1993), 5:148-49.

25. Maistre, *St. Petersburg Dialogues,* 6:184ff.

26. Maistre, *St. Petersburg Dialogues,* 11:325f.

of divine providence. It is not the result of deliberation. It cannot be written nor created a priori. A written constitution only codifies already existing dispositions and is dependent on the unwritten constitution, in which the very spirit of a people is incorporated.[27] Once the written constitution fails to faithfully reflect the unwritten, the nation is at an end.

Bonald and Maistre, in spite of their hatred of the Revolution and their pessimism, which expresses itself in paradoxical and jarring statements,[28] were still influenced to some extent by Enlightenment optimism. To encounter this tradition at its most radical, one must pass to Spain and the works of Don Juan Donoso Cortés (1809-1853), Marqués de Valdegamas. A onetime devotee of Francophile liberalism and sympathetic to the Revolution, he passed through the crucible of personal loss and revolutionary upset (1848) to emerge a chastened, strongly religious conservative. From the gray eminence of Spanish politics — orator, writer, diplomat — he transcended the intrigues of the Spanish court to become a major figure in European matters.

De Maistre had loudly proclaimed that the remedy for the chaos birthed by the Revolution was the Pope and the executioner. Donoso presented his analysis of the situation in his 'Discourse on Dictatorship' delivered in the Cortes on January 4, 1849. He states simply and starkly that history does not move forward irremediably. At present it is receding, lapsing into a new, more terrible paganism which eventually will spawn the most monstrous despotism ever experienced in the world.

His argument is that humanity is subject to only two restraints. One restraint is internal — religion and conscience; one is external — law and force. The more religion and its mandates become interiorized to become principles of conduct the less necessary is external restraint. Conversely, to the extent that religion loses its hold on conscience, external restraint, force, is obliged to take up the slack. This is the situation which prevails at

27. Gilson, Langan, and Maurier, *Recent Philosophy,* 721n.22.
28. "An occult and terrible law demanding human blood" . . . "the executioner: this 'sublime being' is the cornerstone of society." . . . "The remedy for disorder will be pain." Though all these passages were taken from *St. Petersburg Dialogues* (7:211-12; 207; 9:272), they are representative of both Maistre's and Bonald's thought at their most exalted.

present.[29] The downward path of history, Donoso indicates, can be halted only provisionally by delaying actions, usually taking the form of dictatorships. The descent will then continue until history issues into the End Times so dramatically portrayed in Scripture.

In his next major discourse, that on Europe, Donoso presented, in a rather sketchy fashion, a novel theory of history in which modifications of religious belief produce modifications in the political and social orders. Here, a positive stage is followed by a negative stage. In the positive, Christianity makes three affirmations: God exists, God is personal, God is sovereign. This corresponds to traditional Christian monarchy. The negative stage is marked by three negations: God reigns but does not govern, God exists but is not a person, God does not exist. Theism is followed by deism, deism by pantheism, and pantheism by atheism. This is to say, traditional monarchy gives way to constitutional monarchy, this to republicanism based on universal suffrage, and republicanism to anarchy.[30] Each, in turn, produces a different type of society, a different variation on the theme of humanity.

Following Bonald and Maistre, the religious domain is central, its variations duly reflected in the subsidiary realms of politics and society. In 1850, Donoso viewed Europe as poised between pantheism and atheism, between republicanism and anarchy, and did not hold out hope for the future.[31] A cataclysm was approaching which would be generated by the convergence of three events: the dissolution of permanent armies, massive socialist expropriation, and the union of the Slav nations under the Russian banner. Russia would impose God's punishment on the world, and then it too would succumb, infected by the moribund European civilization it had conquered.[32] This good-natured Jeremiah, as Guizot called Donoso, saw a veritable ocean of blood and the advent of the age of the

---

29. Donoso Cortés, "Discurso sobre la Dictadura." *Obras Completas de Don Juan Donoso Cortés,* ed. Carlos Valverde, SJ (Madrid: BAC, 1970), 2:315-16. Cf. my *Donoso Cortés: Cassandra of the Age* (Grand Rapids: Eerdmans, 1995).

30. Donoso Cortés, "Discurso sobre Europa." *Obras,* 2:458-59.

31. Donoso Cortés, "Discurso sobre Europa," 460.

32. Donoso Cortés, *Ensayo sobre el Catolicismo, el Liberalismo, y el socialismo. Obras,* 2: 530-31.

masses prompted by the exacerbations of democracy, centralization, and mechanization abetted by novel inventions. This would destroy all autonomous political bodies and effectively reduce the individual to a fragile atom facing a monolithic state. This would be taken to its radical extreme.

Both Maistre and Donoso struck a responsive note in the mind of Orestes Brownson (1803-1875), author, editor, orator, a New England Yankee converted to Roman Catholicism. In his major work, *The American Republic,* following Maistre, he proposed that the key to modern history resides in the struggle between the unwritten and the written constitution. The former is the foundational constitution of the American people as a sovereign community. The latter originates in law and presupposes the existence of the nation.[33] He embellished the theme to make an invaluable contribution to American political thought.

Donoso's influence on Brownson was muted in spite of his great admiration for the Spaniard's work. Brownson stopped short of radical pessimism. He did not discard progress, of which he had been an avid defender, but, towards the end of his life limited the range of progress to the period between the sixth and sixteenth centuries and attributed it to the influence of the church.[34] The following centuries he viewed with disdain. The spiritual had been subordinated to the material, the church to the state, and consequently true progress was arrested and decline had set in. Although sympathetic to the view that the historical spiral was heading downhill, never formulated this in a definitive manner.

Pessimism was not limited to Roman Catholic ultramontanes. It is also found to a fascinating degree in the speculations of two members of the illustrious Adams family, the brothers Henry (1838-1918) and Brooks (1848-1927). Their views were tied by links of iron to the thought and fortunes of their grandfather, John Quincy Adams, the sixth president of the United States. The doubts that haunted him regarding the existence of God which he could neither silence nor expel cast a chilling shadow over his grandchildren. Brooks spoke of a betrayal by God which affected even

---

33. Orestes Brownson, *The American Republic* (1865). *The Works of Orestes A. Brownson,* ed. Henry F. Brownson (Detroit: Thorndike House, 1882-1887), 18:74, 81f., 113. Cf. my *Orestes Brownson: Sign of Contradiction* (Wilmington: ISI Books, 1999).

34. Brownson, "The Primeval Man Not a Savage." *Works,* 9:472, 474-75.

the American people.[35] It seems that God had failed to honor his part of the compact.

Henry Adams was the cultivated gadfly of the salons of the gilded age. His erudition, curiosity, and social status, in which he delighted, combined with an intellectual puckishness, made him unique. He was a great admirer of the Middle Ages, fascinated by the wonders of Chartres and Mont-Saint-Michel while harboring an almost fundamentalist naiveté regarding Catholic theology — possibly inherited from his Puritan ancestors. He read Marx and found him impressively wrongheaded. His scientific interests and medieval studies supported his claim to be "a dilution of a mixture of Lord Kelvin and St. Thomas Aquinas."[36]

His vision regarding the course of history is forbidding. Modernity is the culmination of a lengthy process of degradation moving towards a variety of socialism which would rot together with civilization. Once man turned from the medieval ideal of spiritual power — the Virgin — to the modern ideal of physical power — the Dynamo — his doom was sealed. As Adams nicely put it, in the contemporary world only the "whirl" was left! Adams regarded progress as sheer nonsense, humorously observing that "the progress of evolution from President Washington to President Grant was alone enough to upset Darwin."[37] Since the Middle Ages, when human activity reached its greatest intensity with the Crusades and cathedrals, vitality has waned.

Inheriting his grandfather's religious doubts, Henry Adams stated that were God to exist it would be possible for humanity to advance towards perfection. Progress requires a principle of unity. But as he very well might not exist, humanity hurtles into the oblivion of eternal night and endless space, sinking into the chaos of which he forms a part.[38] This bleak finale of the human race is furthered by rampaging democracy — an infinite mass of conflicting minds resolved into a vapor — advancing in the direction of "social war" or "massacre."

35. John Quincy Adams, *Memoirs* (v. 235); Henry Adams, *The Degradation of the Democratic Dogma* (New York: The Macmillan Co., 1919), 32.

36. Cited by Russell Kirk, *The Conservative Mind* (South Bend: Gateway, 1978), 314.

37. Henry Adams, *The Education of Henry Adams* (Boston, 1918), 266.

38. Henry Adams, *Degradation,* 101; Kirk, *Conservative Mind,* 317.

In a dense piece, "The Rule of Phase Applied to History," Adams applied the laws of physics to those governing history, attempting to chart the different stages of the process of decadence which characterizes the modern age. He distinguishes three phases: (1) Mechanical — beginning about 1600 AD and reaching its climax in the 1870s; (2) Electrical — which is restricted to the years between 1900 and 1917; and (3) Ethereal — an indeterminate tomorrow which leads to social rot and decline.[39] An ingenious and puzzling account. Brooks Adams was at one with Henry in predicting the decline and fall of civilization but stressed economic factors to a greater extent. In the study of history, he noted the "great gulf" separating economic development from the development of the imagination. The imagination is stimulated by mystery and produces priests and soldiers. The economic, "where energy chooses money as its vent," begets materialism and generates, as its highest product, "the usurer and his gross culture."[40] With the Reformation, the soldier and priest were overpowered, the imaginative type passed away and the monied type possessed the world. This radical change takes place when:

> Energy ceases to vent through the imagination, and takes the form of capital; hence, as civilizations advance, the imaginative temperament tends to disappear, while the economic instinct is fostered, and thus substantially new varieties of men come to possess the world.[41]

What occurs? The family disintegrates. Marriage is debased. The population fuses into a compact mass. Consolidation reaches its apex. Disintegration approaches. Henry, in a letter to Brooks, suggests that mankind's next effort "is more likely to be one of disintegration, with Russia, for the eccentric, on one side, and America on the other." He claims, "Let there be God!" With this we leave the Adamses.[42]

39. Henry Adams, *Degradation,* 267-311.
40. Brooks Adams, *The Law of Civilization and Decay* (London: Macmillan, 1898), 69, 89.
41. Brooks Adams, *Law of Civilization,* 297.
42. Cited in Henry Adams, *Degradation,* 98-99; Brooks Adams, *Law of Civilization,* 383.

The present chapter has attempted to show how the reaction to the French Revolution led (though often hesitantly and with backward glances) to the rejection of progress and its utopian sequelae. Coupled with disenchantment with the Revolution's aftermath and the revival of a strong Roman Catholic presence, this led to a pessimistic if realistic assessment of history and its development. Although the attempts of the Traditionalists and their confreres lacked major intellectual resonance, they represented a style of thought and a psychological type which tends to come to the surface with periodic regularity and is not lacking in grandeur and pathos. In the wake of Traditionalism it remained for Karl Marx to reinstate progress on a rigorous basis within an irreligious context.

CHAPTER 10

Karl Marx: Revolutionary Praxis
as the Road to Utopia

We recognize one science, and one only, history.

Karl Marx (A crossed-out sentence
of an unpublished book)

The road to Karl Marx is strewn with corpses . . . of those who prepared the way, of those who attempted to block his course, and of those who inherited his patrimony. As Raymond Aron has observed, "Marx has several points of contact with Machiavelli. Both are more aware of what divides than what unites men. Both are realists although Marx's realism, unlike Machiavelli's, forms a part of the philosophy of history that, despite everything, deserves to be called optimistic."[1] Marx concentrated on institutions, Machiavelli on man. Marx traced the development of the forces of production. Machiavelli described the struggle of princes. Marx elaborated an economic philosophy of history; Machiavelli a political philosophy.

Machiavelli did not entertain the promise of a radically new future as did Marx who believed that history carries within itself the promise of re-

1. Raymond Aron, *Politics and History,* trans. and ed. Miriam B. Conant (New Brunswick: Transaction, 1984), 91.

demption. "Marx," Aron urges, "stands as the prophet of our time, in which economics, the forces of production, takes on the form of fate."[2] The fact that his thought was progressive, practical, and dialectical made it unique and distinguished it from his precursors, opponents, and even some of his disciples.

To substantiate Aron's dicta it will be necessary to review the thinkers who adumbrated or influenced Marx's thought and then turn to those texts germane to the topic under consideration, the *German Ideology* and *Communist Manifesto* at the forefront. The massive amount of interpretation, commentary, and ensuing controversy elicited by his work will be touched on selectively. Our point of departure will be a thinker who can serve as a bridge between the radically different worlds of Traditionalism and radical Socialism. To choose J. P. Proudhon (1809-65) is hardly arbitrary as he was both excoriated by Donoso Cort Cortés and praised by Karl Marx.

An acute but eccentric mind, Proudhon vaulted from studying Hebrew and annotating Scripture to advocating a struggle to the death against God. Religion, he maintained, was a "vampire" devouring humanity. God is merely the ghost of our conscience, "anti-libéral, anti-civilateur, anti-humain."[3] Belief in God is the greatest obstacle to progress. Works such as *What Is Property?*, *The Philosophy of Poverty,* and *Justice in the Revolution and the Church* cut a swath in European consciousness and influenced many, not excluding Marx. Reacting against the hyper-rationalism of his milieu, Proudhon labeled professional philosophers as "people who work at the absurd business of selling the Absoluté.[4] He suggested that philosophy be displaced from the individual and speculative to the collective and practical.

His status was not diminished by an unfortunate tendency to hold conflicting positions simultaneously, railing against private property and communism, despotism and universal suffrage. Marx first presented the major elements of his thought in the *Poverty of Philosophy,* a polemical

2. Aron, *Politics and History,* 92-93f., 101.

3. Karl Lowith. *Meaning in History* (Chicago: Univ. of Chicago Press, 1949), 63-65, 232; Henri de Lubac, *Proudhon et le christiainsme* (Paris: Editions du Seuil, 1945).

4. Emile Bréhier, *Historia de a Filosofía,* trad. Demetrio Nuñez (Buenos Aires: Editorial Sudamericana, 1962), 3:483.

work directed against Proudhon's *Philosophy of Poverty*. The latter in the *Communist Manifesto* was characterized as an example of the bourgeois socialism which favors "the existing state of society minus its revolutionary and decentralizing elements . . . a bourgeoisie without a proletariat."[5] Yet Marx spent an entire night discussing the Hegelian dialectic with him and Bakunin and praised him in the *Holy Family* (1845).[6] Though he regarded Proudhon as a mind inferior to Saint-Simon and Fourier, Marx realized he had advanced beyond them, an advance he later compared to that of Feuerbach over Hegel.

Moreover, Marx recalled that it was Proudhon who raised the objection against Comte that the finite dimensions of the earth would not admit of a right to property.[7] When Marx and Engels were setting up a network of communist correspondence committees and Proudhon was asked to represent Paris, he responded with surprising prescience:

> Let us not set ourselves up as the masters of a new intolerance, let us not rise up as the apostles of a new religion, even though the religion be one of logic or reason.[8]

Proudhon even made a contribution to the philosophy of history by enlarging the Joachimist triad (Ages of the Father, Son, and Holy Spirit) into a quaternity based on epoch-making crises. The first was effected by Jesus and attained equality before God. The second crisis was brought about by the Reformation and Descartes: it resulted in equality before Reason. The third, equality before the Law, was generated by the French Revolution. The fourth and final crisis, which will bring complete equality, is advancing on the horizon.[9]

---

5. Karl Marx and Friedrich Engels, *Basic Writings on Politics and Philosophy*, ed. Lewis S. Feuer (Garden City: Anchor Books, 1959), 35-36.

6. David McLellan, *The Thought of Karl Marx: An Introduction* (New York: Harper Torchbooks, 1974), 17.

7. Eric L. Hobsbawm, "Marx, Engels and Pre-Marxian Socialism," from *The History of Marxism*, ed. E. L. Hobsbawm (Bloomington: Indiana Univ. Press, 1982), 1:15; Nicola Badaloni, "Marx and the Quest for Communist Liberty," from *History of Marxism*, 1:146.

8. Cited by P. Haubtmann, *Marx et Proudhon* (Paris, 1957), 57.

9. Lowith, *Meaning in History*, 63-65.

Hegel's influence on Marx was, of course, enormous, though it is difficult to determine with exactitude. Exaggerations are rife in the literature. The stage was set when the young Marx wrote his father from Berlin (1837) that he had chained himself more and more firmly to Hegel, this in spite of his "grotesque craggy melody." He believed his own task was "to bring down the Hegelian idea to the level of things . . . to replace speculative idealism with a philosophy of action which reconciles life and philosophy in an authentic way."[10] Although he later became disenchanted with Hegel to some extent, Marx's thought was never to jettison its Hegelian scaffolding.

Nestled under Hegel's gigantic shadow were the Young Hegelian radicals who Marx courted, emulated, rejected, and attacked. They were an exceptionally vocal and idiosyncratic group. Christianity was a favorite target. D. F. Strauss (1808-74) in his *Life of Jesus* asserted that creative power must arise from within not from without the world. Bruno Bauer (1809-82), Marx's friend and teacher, denied the historicity and divinity of Christ, proposing radical atheism.[11] Arnold Ruge (1803-80), the editor of three influential *Jahrbücher*, was perhaps the first to realize that once the dialectic was detached from the Hegelian system it would lead to radical conclusions.[12]

The catalogue has yet to be terminated. Max Stirner (1806-56), whose principal work, translated as *The Ego and Its Own*, was indebted to Hobbes and Machiavelli, went one step further than Feuerbach, who maintained that man had created God in his own image, by proposing that the individual ego had created man in its own image. In his *Historical Reflections* he probed the place of ethnicity in the movement of history, proposing that the Negro race corresponds to mankind's infancy, the Asian to its youth, and the Caucasian to its maturity.[13] Marx wrote a book on Stirner which remained unpublished. Excepting Hegel, the most per-

10. Jean Hyppolite, *Studies on Marx and Hegel,* trans. John O'Neill (New York: Basic Books, 1969), 93-94.
11. Cited by Sidney Hook, *From Hegel to Marx* (New York: Columbia Univ. Press, 1994), 81-84, 93f.
12. Hook, *Hegel to Marx,* 129.
13. Pierre Vilar, "Marx and the Concept of History," from *History of Marxism,* 1:67.

vasive influence on Marx was exercised by Ludwig Feuerbach (1804-72). Although it would later be caricatured by Stirner, Marx and Engels welcomed his *The Essence of Christianity* (1841) as a new and exciting revelation. Marx addressed the Young Hegelians with heavy-handed humor: "There is no other way for you to truth and freedom except through the bath of fire [Feuerbach]: Feuerbach is the purgatory of the present."[14] (Perhaps to enter into the 'heaven' of Marxism?) Feuerbach himself believed that his devastating critique of religion marked a turning point in the history of thought. It certainly provided the point of departure for much future speculation. Marx broke with him in the *German Ideology* while defending him against the attacks of Stirner and Bauer. The *Theses on Feuerbach* was the definitive refutation. It is the eleventh of these theses which sounds the clarion call: "The philosophers have only interpreted the world in various ways; the point, however, is to change it."[15]

Although others belonging to the radical milieu could be mentioned (Blanc, Lassalle, Hess, Bakunin, and others) it is better to cut to the quick and study the essentials of Marx's thought and the principles that support it. At the center is the lesson he received from "the most illustrious saint in the philosophical calendar" — Prometheus. This belief, in Bloch's words, "that man is the highest being for man, and hence with the categorical imperative to overthrow all conditions in which man is a degraded, enslaved, abandoned and wretched creature,"[16] became his mission. The fulfillment of this charge seemed to be emerging slowly, laboriously, *seriatim*. In a letter to Ruge, Marx observes that the world has long possessed in dream form something of which it need only become conscious of in order to possess it in reality.[17] In spite of its obvious He-

14. Hook, *Hegel to Marx*, 118.

15. Marx and Engels, *Basic Writings*, 243-45. Marx's principal criticisms: Feuerbach overestimates theory, does not grasp the significance of revolutionary activity, does not realize that the human essence is not an abstraction but an ensemble of social relations, and does not stress the revolutionizing of the secular basis of the religious world that he had uncovered.

16. Ernst Bloch, *On Karl Marx*, trans. John Maxwell (New York: Herder & Herder, 1976), 22.

17. Bloch, *On Karl Marx*, 27-28.

gelian intimations, the temptation persists to interpret his statement in Freudian terms.

In any case, for Marx a purely rational analysis is peripheral to the real analysis, what Lukacs calls "the descent into the real, underlying, objective foundations of the movement of philosophy."[18] Marx tended to view Hegel's *Phenomenology* as a refracted anticipation of his own thought: "Hegel views the self-creation of man as a process . . . . He grasps the nature of labor and understands objective man . . . as the product of his own labor."[19] No wonder the *Phenomenology* has been considered by scholars as required reading for the comprehension of *Capital*.

Though it is possible to list Campanella among his precursors — Marx planned to include the *City of the Sun* in the abortive 'Library of Foreign Socialist Writers' he projected with Engels and Hess (1845)[20] — more to the point is Rousseau (1712-1778), whose persistent underscoring of equality established him as an icon with the Jacobin left. Even more important was Charles Darwin (1809-1882) whose Beagle voyage and subsequent publication of *The Origin of Species* and *The Descent of Man* created the impression, in the words of T. H. Huxley, that "teleology, as commonly understood, had received its deathblow."[21] Also welcomed by Marx was Darwin's support for the premise he established whereby the unity of natural and human history is seen to be intrinsic, not a grand design imposed by a Deity.[22]

Engel's oration at Marx's graveside, praising him for discovering the law of evolution in human history as Darwin had in organic nature, makes the point. Marx did not want to detach progress from evolution. Writing to Engels he faulted Darwin for making progress only an accidental by-product.[23] In fact, Marx did not deal directly with historical

18. Georg Lukacs, *The Young Hegel* (Cambridge: MIT Press, 1976), xiv-xv.

19. Cited in Lukacs, *Young Hegel*, xxvii.

20. Hobsbawm, "Marx, Engels," 1:1.

21. T. H. Huxley, *Lectures and Essays* (London: People's Library, 1922), 178-79.

22. Lawrence Krader, "Evolution, Revolution, and the State," from *History of Marxism*, 1: 196.

23. Eric Hobsbawm, "What Do Historians Owe to Karl Marx?" from *On History* (New York: New Press, 1997), 50. Marx to Engels (August 7, 1866). Cited in ibid., 285n.13.

change until 1844. As McLellan indicates, it was in Brussels in late 1845 that Marx and Engels first set down what Marx, in 1859, called the "guiding thread" of his studies, *The German Ideology*.[24] There is little doubt that Darwin's theories played a part in reinforcing Marx's views and elevating the doctrine and cult of progress to a higher and more rigorous level.

A nutshell, however inadequate, of Marx's life and work, can be obtained by merely scanning the headings corresponding to the second part of Jean-Yves Calvez's *La penseé de Karl Marx:*[25]

(1818-1836) — Liberation from Religion;
(1836-1843) — Liberation from Philosophy;
(1843-1845) — Liberation from the Primacy of the Political;
(1845-1848) — Theory joins Practice;
(1848-1870) — Together with the Worker's Movement;
(1870-1883) — The End of the International and Future Anticipations.

This is merely a skeletal outline, a mere index, of the life of a man with uncommon talents, which demands filling in. A unique character in which the clash of extremes often emerged undomesticated, Marx was able to meld disciplined thought and visceral emotion to produce an explosive ideology of still unexplored possibilities.

A descendent of generations of rabbis, Karl Marx studied law at the University of Bonn. When he transferred to Berlin he fell under the prevailing spell of Hegel, wrote a thesis, "The Difference Between the Natural Philosophies of Democritus and Epicurus" (favoring Epicurus), which gained a doctorate from Jena. At an early age he gave evidence of catholic tastes. His daughter Eleanor indicates that while Marx's father read Voltaire and Racine with him, the Baron — his father-in-law — tilted him towards Homer and Shakespeare, who remained his favorite

24. David McLellan, "The Materialistic Concept of History," from *History of Marxism,* 1:43.

25. Jean-Yves Calvez, *El pensamiento de Carlos Marx,* version española de Florentino Trapero (Madrid: Taurus, 1966), 741.

authors.[26] His attention turned to journalism; writing his first article for Ruge's *Deutsche Jahrbücher* (1842) led to a checkered career that would end ultimately in exile. At the time he proposed to transform the criticism of heaven, so admirably carried out by Feuerbach, into the criticism of earth: "History has for long enough been resolved into superstition: we now resolve superstition into history."[27]

The notion of the proletariat as the "material weapon" of philosophy begins to be elaborated: the self-conscious independent movement of the immense majority, who, having suffered the complete loss of humanity, can only redeem itself by a complete redemption of humanity. Alienation is treated in the *Paris Manuscripts* (1844). It lies at the very root of the capitalist system. The abolition of private property is proposed as the final solution to the riddle of history.[28] Between 1845 and 1848 Marx wrote three important works, *The Holy Family, The German Ideology,* and *The Poverty of Philosophy,* the first two relevant to the study at hand. By the time of *The Communist Manifesto* (1848), he was in revolutionary Paris, charting his course for London. Ferdinand Lassalle, the "jüdische nigger," started a collection to finance the trip.[29]

Life in England was bleak. The Marxes lived in a small flat in Soho for six years, most of the time on the verge of starvation. Family tragedies mounted. Between 1855 and 1860 they lost three of their children. His intense study at the British Museum continued to the point that in 1858 Lassalle spoke of him as "a Hegel turned economist, a Ricardo turned Socialist."[30] The death of his mother and a friend improved his financial position and the family moved to more ample quarters. The first volume of *Capital* was completed in April 1867. The First International, which he had founded in 1864, was brought to an end in 1872 because of divergences with Bakunin. In the interim the star of Prussia had risen notably, defeating Austria in 1866 and France in 1870. During the last decade of

26. Eleanor Marx on Karl Marx. *Die Neue Zeit,* 1883, p. 441.

27. Karl Marx, *Early Texts,* ed. David McLellan (New York: Oxford Univ. Press, 1971), 91.

28. Marx, *Early Texts,* 148.

29. McLellan, *Thought of Karl Marx,* 42.

30. Lassalle to Marx (May 12, 1850).

his life Marx languished, too ill for any extended work. He died on March 14, 1883.

Marx's thought marks a watershed. Its roots reach back to Joachim of Fiore and further, to the inspired utterances of the Old Testament prophets. Containing borrowings from Hegel, the Young Hegelians and others, his thought has exercised a peculiar fascination on philosophers, revolutionaries, and scholars. It has excited the interest of minds as diverse as Bloch, Hyppolite, Berdyaev, Garaudy, and Althusser,[31] not to mention lighting the fuse of the historical upset brought to a head by V. I. Lenin (1870-1924). Hobsbawm cannot be dismissed as an overzealous partisan when he declares: "I can only assert my conviction that Marx's approach is still the only one which enables us to explain the entire span of history, and forms the most fruitful starting-place for modern discussion."[32] Ernst Bloch is more enthusiastic: Marx has provided, he urges, a new version of the doctrine of man as the measure of all things that is paving the way to the actual, concrete Utopia.[33]

The philosophy of history is all-encompassing, including all of Marx's major ports of call: economics, dialectic, alienation, labor, revolution and the society of the future. Its point of departure is Hegel's power of the negative, the tension between any present state of affairs and what will succeed it, that which it is already becoming. Dialectics is the law of matter in motion. In this dialectical progression each stage marks an advance beyond its predecessor. Standing Hegel's dialectic on its head, Marx considers the changing economic basis of society — and the classes to which it gives rise — the key to grasping the unfolding of history.[34] History can be understood as a process in which new needs are created as the result of material changes instituted to fulfill the old. The mode of production is then the way in which nature is mediated by man, the basic fact that an analysis of society must take into account.

---

31. Hyppolite, *Studies on Marx and Engels;* Ernst Bloch, *On Karl Marx;* Roger Garaudy, *La Théorie Materialiste de la connaissance* (Paris: PUF, 1954); Nikolai Berdyaev, *Le marxisme et la religion* (Paris: Edicion Le Sers, 1932); L. Althusser, *For Marx* (London, 1970).

32. E. Hobsbawm, "Historians," 155.

33. Bloch, *On Karl Marx,* 152, 168.

34. McLellan, *Karl Marx,* 122.

Marx proposed that asiatic, ancient, feudal, and modern bourgeois modes of production were progressive stages in the formation of society. In *The German Ideology* he described historical movement by means of progressive forms of ownership. The first is tribal — hunting, fishing, and at its highest, agriculture — employing an elementary division of labor. The second is the ancient communal system: several tribes are amalgamated into a village and private property begins to develop. The third is feudal, in which the country predominates and antagonism to towns develops, with a rudimentary division of labor.[35] At this point, on the border of incipient capitalism, the account ceases.

One of the most famous propositions of the *Communist Manifesto* states that "the history of all hitherto existing society is the history of class struggle."[36] Exploiter and exploited face each other at every stage of history, within societies which are arranged, up to the present, into diverse orders and classes. In the words of *The German Ideology:*

> History is nothing but the succession of the separate generations, each of which exploits the material, the capital funds, the productive forces handed down to it by all preceding generations, and thus, on the one hand, continues the traditional activity in completely changed circumstances, and, on the other, modifies the old circumstances with a completely changed activity.[37]

History is based on the mode of production which generates civil society in its various stages and underlies the formation of consciousness: "Man's ideas, views and conceptions, in one word, man's consciousness, change with every change in the conditions of his material existence, in his social relations, and in his social life."[38] Because of this, the ruling ideas of a given society have always been those of the ruling class. But the modern bourgeoisie has simplified matters by whittling down the orders

35. Karl Marx, *The German Ideology,* trans. W. Lough, ed. C. J. Arthur (New York: International Publishers, 1974), 44-46.
36. Marx and Engels, *Basic Writings,* 7.
37. Marx, *German Ideology,* 57.
38. Marx and Engels, *Basic Writings,* 7-8, 26.

and classes of the past into two great opposing camps: the owners of the means of production and the wage-laborers, which is to say, the bourgeoisie and the proletariat.

Capitalism has shattered all feudal and patriarchal ties between men, reducing the nexus between men to "callous cash payment."[39] It has replaced a multiplicity of freedoms by one solitary, absolute freedom — free trade. It is incessantly revolutionizing the instruments of production, drawing everybody and everything into its orbit. However, its great success has released productive forces that are too powerful to control, a situation that generates the proletariat, its executioner. Marx's aim is clear: "the formation of the proletariat into a class, overthrow of bourgeois supremacy, conquest of political power by the proletariat."[40]

And what of the future? Marx shied away from prognostication as a weakness proper to utopian sentimentalists like Hermann Kriege, who aspired to combat poverty by means of "the dew of sentiment suffused with love."[41] Nevertheless, it would seem that a vault into the future is required once his genealogy of economics has arrived at the self-immolation of capitalism and mankind stands on the precipice of a new era. Marx looked forward to a future in which man would slough away the contradictions holding him captive and become authentically human.

Though he spoke of the Dictatorship of the Proletariat as an interim period in which prehistory would give way to authentic history, its extent remains nebulous. Doubtless, Marx believed that during this period even alienation — which appeared in *Capital* under the chilling title of "Fetishism of Commodities" — would ultimately disappear. This is of particular importance as the human relation that assumes fantastic form as a relation between things actually transfers control of the historical process from man to the inhuman power of capital.[42] As the state is an expression of alienation, it follows that its most essential part, the bureaucracy, must be abolished: "Freedom consists in converting the state from an organ superior to society into one completely subordinate to

39. Marx and Engels, *Basic Writings*, 8-9.
40. Marx and Engels, *Basic Writings*, 20.
41. Bloch, *On Karl Marx*, 19.
42. Karl Marx, *Das Kapital* 1:72, 177; McLellan, *Karl Marx*, 108ff.

it."[43] The political revolution will issue into the social revolution — the definitive revolution — which will bring about general emancipation. The proletariat, in making the revolution, transforms itself.

Saint-Simon predicted that a transition would take place from the government of people to the administration of things. Marx spoke of the 'transcendence' or 'abolition' of the state, describing the society to come as an association. Distinguishing between *constant desires* (which exist under all circumstances) and *relative desires* (which owe their origin to a particular form of society), he maintained that in a communist society the first would be modified and given the opportunity to develop normally, while the latter would be eradicated.[44] Production and exchange would be modified to ensure satisfaction. With adequate free time, the individual would develop into a 'universal individual' able to enjoy wholly different activities almost at will.

The Dictatorship of the Proletariat is the port of entry for the resolution of contradictions and the building of the 'new world' as well as the crucible from which authentic history would emerge. Returning to the interim period between capitalism and communism we must ask: is it a brief hiatus or a lengthy period? This remains a point of controversy. The weight of opinion, buttressed by the more than eight decades that separates us from the Russian Revolution, tilts towards the second option. However, given Marx's abhorrence of teleology, it would be unwise to affirm that the 'communist association' of the future is the final goal of history.

In his later works Marx deliberately views history in reverse order, taking developed capitalism as his point of departure. This brings certain peculiarities of Marx's method to light. The present is his center of attention. The past is telescoped and treated as the burial ground of principles he unearths. The future is left opaque. He differed from the veritable menagerie of radicals who populated the Europe of his day principally because of his opposition to both desiccated speculation and blind revolutionary violence. He melded both in a superior synthesis, praxis, both

43. McLellan, *Karl Marx*, 86.
44. McLellan, *Karl Marx*, 216.

philosophical doctrine and revolutionary movement, thought joined to political action.

Marx's thought, albeit often modified or extended, has enjoyed an importance that can be described only as earth-shattering, comparable only to the irruptions caused by the major religions. Far more than an intellectual tour-de-force, it possesses a visceral strength that can change hearts as well as minds, lead to conversion and form zealots. Only the vicissitudes of time prevented Marx from personifying Machiavelli's armed prophet, a role filled in part by Lenin. Ernst Bloch waxes enthusiastic: "It is given to all to spread such an idea — the human structure of Marxism — as reality on the face of the earth."[45] His doctrine echoes on a secular level the scriptural command: *"Ite, incendite omnia."*

Marx's writings (as well as those of Engels) have acquired the status of classics, even that of Scripture to true believers, wherever they form the nucleus of the official ideology. Until recently well over a billion people lived under regimes which pledged allegiance to Marxist doctrine. Intramural conflict has been rife from the beginning and seems to augment in tandem with the divisions, political and theoretical, within the Socialist bloc. Even within the Soviet Union, in 1938, the orthodox Stalinist interpretation, which was then promulgated, made some of Marx's writings (those of the early 1840s) appear heterodox.[46] For over one hundred and fifty years since *The Communist Manifesto,* Marxism has taken on the accouterments of a religion with its dogmas, authorities, and labyrinthine squabbles. Proudhon's 1846 admonition begins to take on the character of prophecy.

---

45. Bloch, *On Karl Marx,* 15.

46. Hobsbawm, "The Future of Marx and Engels' Writings," from *History of Marxism,* 1:334.

CHAPTER 11

Friedrich Nietzsche
and the Twilight of History

According to Friedrich Nietzsche, in an age without genuine culture the philosopher is like a comet, incalculable and terrifying.[1] He could not have described himself more exactly. Nietzsche was excoriated and in turn excoriated his age unmercifully. It was, he said, shrouded in humbug, distorted and degenerate: "The world has never been more worldly, never poorer in love and goodness; everything, art and science included, serves the coming barbarian."[2] He was a veritable comet, a terrifying anomaly, unique in that he recapitulated the entire epoch initiated by Descartes. Traces of major thinkers are found in Nietzsche's works in mutated form, absorbed within the circulatory system of his thought. He refused to be historically fixed:

> I am of today and of the has-been . . . there is something in me that
> is of tomorrow and of the day-after-tomorrow and of the shall-be.[3]

---

1. Friedrich Nietzsche, *Philosophy in the Tragic Age of the Greeks,* trans. Marianne Cowan (Washington: Regnery Gateway, 1987), 34.
2. Friedrich Nietzsche, *Untimely Meditations,* trans. R. J. Hollingdale (Cambridge: Cambridge Univ. Press, 1983), 148-49.
3. Friedrich Nietzsche, *Thus Spake Zarathustra,* trans. R. J. Hollingdale (Baltimore: Penguin, 1968), 150.

Nietzsche believed that all philosophies have one distinguishing characteristic: personal mood, color.[4] His own mood is dramatic, somber yet luminous, not unlike that of the Old Testament prophets. His style is visionary, his colors scream! As he wrote Overbeck: "You complain that I use screaming colors . . . perhaps I have a nature which screams."[5] He made ample use of aphorisms, peaks from which the fertile valleys of speculation could be discerned. A person who writes in aphorisms "does not want to be read, he wants to be learned by heart"[6] — as an authoritative teacher propounding a new gospel, as a prophet!

The religious tone came naturally to a man whose family had been Lutheran for generations, his father a minister, his grandfather the author of a tract, *Gamaliel,* advocating the perennial survival of Christianity.[7] Even more than Saint Augustine, Nietzsche can be understood only when profiled against the backdrop of his life. Massive pressures from the unconscious and wilds turns of the imagination melded with a sensitivity that can only be characterized as pathological. This made him a superb writer and psychologist, an extravagant thinker and a poor stick of a man. It accounts for his many eccentricities, a penchant for elevating the personal to the monumental. He could have been writing about himself when he wrote that the 'Schopenhauerian man'

> will have to be an enemy to those he loves and to the institutions
> which produced him; he may not spare men or things, even though
> he suffers when they suffer: he will be misunderstood and for long
> thought an ally of powers he abhors.[8]

As a child Nietzsche was pensive, serious, and religious, raised in a matriarchal household. He attended the venerable Schulpforta, where he abandoned Christianity. From there he went to the universities of Bonn, to

4. Nietzsche, *Philosophy in the Tragic Age,* 23-24.
5. Letter of Aug. 5, 1886. Cited by Karl Jaspers, *Nietzsche,* trans. Charles F. Wallraff and Frederick J. Schmitz (Tuscon: Univ. of Arizona Press, 1966), 87.
6. Nietzsche, *Zarathustra,* 67.
7. Ivo Frenzel, *Friedrich Nietzsche* (New York: Penguin Books, 1967), 8.
8. Nietzsche, *Untimely Meditations,* 153.

study philology, and Leipzig where, in 1866, he gave a series of lectures on Theognis of Megara, later published in the *Rheinisches Museum*.[9] Recommended by Ritschl, the youthful scholar accepted a professorship on the staff of the University of Basel at the age of twenty-four (1869). Nietzsche taught there for ten years and wrote *The Birth of Tragedy,* which, in turn, led to his exclusion from the philological establishment. At the time his interest in historical studies was furthered by his acquaintance with historian Jacob Burckhardt, who at the time was lecturing on historical greatness.

Never truly healthy, in 1873 his maladies began to burgeon: migraines, eye-problems, stomach disorders, and psychopathological episodes. *Untimely Meditations,* a series of four essays, appeared (1873-1876). Resigning his post at Basel due to his health (1879), Nietzsche began a life of wandering, residing at Venice, Turin, Sils Maria, the French Riviera, and other ports of call. His writing continued: *Human, All Too Human* (1878), *The Joyful Wisdom* (1882), and the *Dawn of Day* (1884), works which culminated in *Thus Spake Zarathustra* (1882-1885), a work he characterized in *Ecce Homo* (1888) as the 'fifth gospel'. Unfortunately, his personal life did not parallel his art, the exceptional sweep of his work. Two efforts in the military ended ingloriously, his dealings with women bordered on the ludicrous, and many of his friendships were jagged. Physical and psychological ailments combined, reaching a crescendo on January 4, 1889, at the Plaza Carlo Alberto in Turin. A massive breakdown was later diagnosed as progressive paralysis. After languishing in a semi-vegetative state for the next decade under the care of his mother, then sister, he lapsed into that "beautiful monstrosity" which is eternity on August 25, 1900.

To arrive at even a minimal understanding of Nietzsche's thought, it is necessary to look behind his many masks and masquerades (of which there are many). Thoughts, he urged, are only shadows of sentiments, always more obscure, empty, and simple.[10] Though masks are more appropriate to the 'mediocre gregarious animal' not to a 'beast of prey' such as himself, they were extensively employed. Every philosophy conceals a philosophy,

9. Frenzel, *Nietzsche,* 25-26.
10. Friedrich Nietzsche, *Joyful Wisdom,* trans. Thomas Common (New York: Frederick Unger, 1960), 1:39, 76-77.

every opinion a hiding place, every word a mask.[11] His major philosophical question was, what is behind the mask of becoming, of appearance? Our question is now, what lies behind Nietzsche's masquerade and how does it relate to the philosophy of history? We must take his relief-like, incomplete presentation, and attempt to think it through to the end.[12]

It is imperative, then, to turn to his precursors and then pass to consideration of the substance of his thought as reflected in the major themes of the Death of God, Will-to-Power, Overman, and Eternal Recurrence. Once interconnected, they lead into his philosophy of history. His first serious enthusiasm was Heraclitus of Ephesus, who convinced him of the impermanence of things: "It is the fault of your myopia, not of the nature of things, if you believe you see land somewhere in the ocean of coming to be and passing away."[13] Nietzsche insisted that law in becoming and play in necessity must be seen in all eternity.[14] Though Being — eternal, immobile, unchanging — seems to be lurking behind Becoming, this is not the case, for Being labors under the disadvantage of not existing. Nothing lies behind the mask of Becoming. Nietzsche will propose that the mask is the face, that Becoming, as he puts it, is the 'lighthouse' that illuminates the sea of history:

Ours is the 'kingdom of Heaven', of change, with Spring and Autumn, winter and summer, and theirs is the 'backworld' — with its gray, frosty, unending mist and shadow.[15]

In this way does he compare the world of Becoming with that of Being by attaching strict necessity to the ancient notion of the 'great year of Becoming', which, like a glass, turns itself over and over again.

Although Nietzsche venerated Spinoza, he turned Spinoza's philoso-

11. Friedrich Nietzsche, *Beyond Good and Evil,* trans. and ed. Marion Faber (Oxford: Oxford Univ. Press, 1998), no. 289, 173.

12. Friedrich Nietzsche, *Human, All Too Human,* trans. R. J. Hollingdale (Cambridge: Cambridge Univ. Press, 1996), no. 178, 92.

13. Nietzsche, *Philosophy in the Tragic Age,* 51-52.

14. Nietzsche, *Philosophy in the Tragic Age,* 68.

15. Nietzsche, *Human, All Too Human,* no. 17, 218.

phy of immanence against him.[16] In place of the *Deus Sive Natura* pervaded by reason and law, he posited a universe in constant flux. Against Spinoza's vision, in which only the particular, the individual, is defective as all is redeemed in the whole, we find the particular ensconced in solitary majesty while the whole is, in effect, dismantled. More important, he takes Spinoza's notion of *conatus* — the essence of a living thing to persevere in existence — to its ultimate, radical conclusion in his doctrine of the Will-to-Power.

Closer at hand is Schopenhauer, who prodded him in the direction of pessimism and asceticism. Nietzsche even attempted self-discipline, retiring at 2 am and rising at 6 am . . . for all of two weeks. Together with Burckhardt, also an admirer of Schopenhauer, he began to attribute the greatest achievements of Hellenic culture to its pessimism. In *Schopenhauer as Educator,* he insisted that one must refuse to "allow existence to resemble a mindless act of chance."[17] Becoming must be rehabilitated. In the same tract he discussed the dangers to which the uncommon man is prone. In what can be taken as a successful attempt at self-analysis, he points out that such men can be driven so deeply into themselves that when they reemerge they do so by means of a volcanic eruption.[18]

If Schopenhauer captivated Nietzsche through the power of his mind, Richard Wagner overpowered him by means of his seductive personality and musical legerdemain. His visits to the Wagners at Tribschen remained engraved in his memory as a paradisiacal interlude in an otherwise tortured life. The composer was a superb self-promoter, convincing Nietzsche that his *Ring des Nibelungen* combined music, drama, poetry, and the plastic arts into a *'Gesamkunst',* a complete work of art that could further the radical transformation of society. This led him to consider further the possibility of effecting a metamorphosis or 'sanctification' of mankind, not, however, in the mass but in the exceptional individual.[19]

16. Yirmiyahu Yovel, *Spinoza and Other Heretics* (Princeton: Princeton Univ. Press, 1989), 104.

17. Nietzsche, *Untimely Meditations,* 128.

18. Nietzsche, *Untimely Meditations,* 140-43.

19. Arthur Herman, *The Idea of Decline in Western History* (New York: The Free Press, 1997), 93.

The *Birth of Tragedy* (1872) and *Richard Wagner in Bayreuth* (1876) were laudatory to an extreme. The *Ring* is the most moral of all pieces of music, its composer applauded for restoring the language of Nature, transfiguring the past and being the herald of a new age.[20] Even after the definite break between the two because of *Parsifal* and its Christian accoutrements, Nietzsche remained under his influence, later censures notwithstanding. Gustav Engel was not far from the mark when he remarked that Nietzsche died of Wagner.[21] Perhaps his innermost desire was expressed in *The Joyful Wisdom:* "Let us believe in our star friendship even if we should be compelled to be earth enemies."[22] An added touch of pathos. The concluding section of *Zarathustra* was completed 'in the same holy hour' that Wagner died in Venice.

Charles Andler presents a veritable catalogue of 'precursors' in the first volume of his *Nietzsche: Sa vie et sa pensée.*[23] At least two merit attention: Burckhardt and Pascal. A highly intelligent eccentric *pace* Nietzsche, Burckhardt considered that European civilization was in crisis. The masses, heirs of the French Revolution, in joining forces with commerce, would ineluctably generate a democratic despotism "which would serve as model for every despotism for all eternity."[24] For his part, Pascal was unique, the supreme example of a profound intellectual conscience wounded by surrendering itself to the dictates of religion. He could have reminded Nietzsche of his own youthful faith and its abandonment, which prepared the way for his 'death of God' jeremiad. Or perhaps Pascal brought to the surface his own profound if idiosyncratic religiosity. Pascal's horror of "the silence of the infinite spaces" reappears in the Eternal Recurrence. And his notion that the finite is annihilated in the presence of the infinite, becoming a pure nothing (*Pensées* #233), must have been painfully present to his mind.

---

20. Nietzsche, *Untimely Meditations,* 198ff., 251ff.

21. Sander L. Gilman, ed., *Conversations with Nietzsche: A Life in the Words of His Contemporaries,* trans. David J. Parent (New York: Oxford Univ. Press, 1987), 127.

22. Nietzsche, *Joyful Wisdom,* no. 279.

23. Charles Andler, *Nietzsche: Sa vie et sa pensée,* 6 vols. (Paris: Bossard, 1920-1931).

24. Herman, *Idea of Decline,* 83-85.

"On the Three Metamorphoses" in *Thus Spake Zarathustra* can, as Lowith has observed, be used as the key to the understanding of "Nietzsche's counter-gospel."[25] Modifying Lowith's interpretation to some extent, the 'thou shalt' of the camel can be said to correspond to scriptural law; the 'I will' of the lion to the nihilism represented by the 'last men'; the 'I am' of the cosmic child to the freedom of the Overman: tradition, rejection of tradition, creative novelty. The process itself is attached to the movement of increasing life, a movement that was frustrated because the depredations of Christianity had made man into the poverty-stricken caricature encountered in the modern world.

"God is dead!" This proclamation of the madman in *The Joyful Wisdom* is dramatic, alarming, and not without pathos. "Is there still an above and a below? Do we not stray, as though in infinite nothingness? . . . Do we not hear the noise of the grave-diggers who are burying God?"[26] Nietzsche was one of the few to appreciate the enormity of this momentous event that had already begun to cast its first shadows. He predicted a long and uninterrupted process of crumbling, destruction, ruin, and overthrow. Nevertheless, the enemy — God — has not been eliminated: "There will perhaps be caves for millenniums yet, in which people will show his shadow — and we still have to overcome his shadow."[27] One might wonder if this shadow was not also present in the cave of his own unconscious.

That Nietzsche's attack on Christianity has such force stems from its being launched from within. He clearly foresaw the tremendous upset that would follow the eclipse of the Christian vision. That is why he attempted (to a believer an incredible blasphemy) to replace it, to find a hole through which he could arrive at 'something'.[28] He castigated Christianity for effecting the daring reversal of those ancient values that had produced a healthy society, of which the Greek philosophers were a faithful reflection, and for endorsing a 'slave morality' unanimous in con-

25. Nietzsche, *Zarathustra*, 54-56. Karl Lowith, *Meaning in History* (Chicago: Univ. of Chicago Press, 1949), 211-12.

26. Nietzsche, *Joyful Wisdom*, 3: no. 125, 157-69.

27. Nietzsche, *Joyful Wisdom*, 3: no. 108, 151.

28. Letter of May 23, 1887. Cited by Jaspers, *Nietzsche*, 120.

demning the ancient world as sinful. The pagan Roman charge of atheism is resuscitated: there is one God is the most godless saying.[29] Scorn is
heaped on that intrusive, petty Divinity who personally knows every little
hair on our heads. However, there is another, more subtle reason for
God's demise. It is the result of the exigencies of Christian morality transferred to the scientific conscience "taking the form of intellectual purity at
any price."[30]

With the death of God the scepter passes to man. Future generations
belong to a higher level of history.[31] In a variation of Vico's *Verum Factum*
principle, Nietzsche urges that although man cannot create a God, he can
create an Overman. He can take his life into his own hands and transform
everything into the humanly conceivable, the humanly evident, the world
formed in the image of man.[32] The path is cleared for the advent of the
Overman: "God has died: now we desire — that the Overman shall
live."[33] In any case, is it necessary that there actually be a God if belief in
the Overman's existence produces the same effect? Is God not superfluous?[34] Christianity has further obfuscated the problem by an eschatology
that forces men to live in fear of the approaching end and makes this end
the goal and completion of world history. But the goal of history cannot
lie in its end, only in its highest exemplars.

Nietzsche's attack extends to those secularized parodies of Christianity that are the boast of the modern world, such as democracy, socialism,
and humanitarianism. He had no sympathy for progress, liberalism,
equal rights, or any of the other shibboleths of modernity. With surprising
acuity, he states, "once spirit was God, then it became man, and now it is
even becoming mob."[35] He lashed out at those "tarantulas" — preachers
of equality — who, prodded by resentment, deal in hidden revenge. He
especially despised socialism as it aspires to the annihilation of the indi-

29. Nietzsche, *Zarathustra*, 201.
30. Nietzsche, *Joyful Wisdom*, 5: no. 357, 308.
31. Nietzsche, *Joyful Wisdom*, 3: no. 125, 168.
32. Nietzsche, *Zarathustra*, 110.
33. Nietzsche, *Zarathustra*, 297.
34. Nietzsche, *Human, All Too Human*, no. 225, 269-70.
35. Nietzsche, *Zarathustra*, 67.

vidual, transforming him into a useful member of the community: "Where the rabble also drinks, all wells are poisoned."[36]

The herd is the negation of life, and consequently the negation of the Will-to-Power. To maintain oneself in existence does not suffice. Life aims at more, at the expansion of power, "the unexhausted, procreating life-will."[37] Philosophy is the most spiritual form of this tyrannical drive and is intent on creating the world in its own image: "You want to create a world before which you can kneel: this is your ultimate hope and intoxication."[38] Man creates the Overman and 'values' *('valeurs'),* a term taken by Nietzsche from the language of artists, to distinguish differences between appearances. Values, as Hannah Arendt suggests, are social commodities that have no significance of their own "and exist only in the ever-changing relativity of social linkages and commerce."[39]

'God is dead' signifies that there is no ultimate norm, no center of truth and intelligibility, and no reality hidden behind the mask of appearance. Moral distinctions vanish. There is no difference in kind between good and evil. Good is sublimated evil. Evil is brutalized good. Hatred, cruelty, and whatever else is called 'evil' belong, in Nietzsche's phrase, "to the conservation of the race."[40] The strongest and most evil spirits have done most to advance humanity. Heroic men are the great pain-givers. On descending to the town for the first time, Zarathustra proclaims: "I teach you the Overman. Man is something that must be overcome. What have you done to overcome him?"[41]

The Overman is the justification of mankind, the great sea in which the 'great contempt' can go under. It vindicates the men of the future and redeems the men of the past. Men must be lured away from the herd. New values must be created and the traditional table of values smashed. Value-creation goes hand in hand with law-breaking: "You solitaries of today, from you . . . shall a chosen people spring, and from this chosen

36. Nietzsche, *Human, All Too Human,* no. 473, 173; *Zarathustra,* 120.
37. Nietzsche, *Zarathustra,* 137.
38. Nietzsche, *Beyond Good and Evil,* no. 9, 15; *Zarathustra,* 136.
39. Hannah Arendt, *Between Past and Future* (New York: Penguin, 1993), 32, 34.
40. Nietzsche, *Joyful Wisdom,* 1: 1, 31ff.
41. Nietzsche, *Zarathustra,* 240-41; 3, 41.

people, an Overman."[42] Kaufmann notes that the term *'Hyperanthropos'* (Overman) was found in Lucian, used by Heinrich Miller in 1664, and later by Herder, Jean Paul, and Goethe.[43] It was also used at the time by certain religious writers referring to Christ. Nietzsche, in the notes that were collated by his sister Elizabeth to comprise the posthumous *Will to Power,* spoke of the ideal as the Roman Emperor with Christ's soul.[44]

Opposed to the Overman is the 'last' or 'ultimate' man who makes everything small — the man who no longer despises himself and remains fixed to his petty mediocrity. He is scarcely a will of the wisp. His race is as long-lasting and inextinguishable as the flea. No herdsman and one herd. Everyone desires the same things. It is a gem of irony that Zarathustra's first discourse presenting the Overman ends with the crowd imploring: "make us into this last man."[45] Nietzsche followed in the wake of Cournot, who believed that man, in organizing everything so as to avoid risk, will become satisfied with a bland happiness and float contentedly on the waters of the trivial.[46] Nietzsche viewed the species as "abstractions made concrete," and "muffled up identical people."[47] The individual, the 'exception,' moves in the opposite direction.

The Death of God, the Will-to-Power, and the Overman coalesce to shed light on Nietzsche's philosophy of history once the Eternal Recurrence is broached, his most important and by far most unsettling doctrine. It came to him in August, 1881, six thousand feet beyond man and time:

> I walked through the forest by the lake of Silvaplana; I stopped near
> a mighty pyramidically heaped block not far from Surlei. Then the
> thought came to me . . . the mightiest thought.[48]

42. Nietzsche, *Zarathustra,* 42, 52; no. 103.

43. Walter Kaufmann, *Nietzsche: Philosopher, Psychologist, Antichrist* (Princeton: Princeton Univ. Press, 1974), 307-8.

44. Cited by Aron, *Politics and History,* trans. M. B. Conant (New Brunswick: Transaction, 1984), 81.

45. Nietzsche, *Zarathustra,* 46-47.

46. Emile Bréhier, *The History of Philosophy,* trans. Wade Baskin (Chicago: Univ. of Chicago Press, 1973), 7, 111.

47. Nietzsche, *Zarathustra,* 84, 86.

48. Jaspers, *Nietzsche,* 357-58.

This mightiest thought had its point of departure in *On the Uses and Disadvantages of History for Life* (1874) in the notion of the supra-historical. As distinguished from the historical and unhistorical, the supra-historical perspective is one for whom the world is finished in every single moment and its goal attained.[49] This is to say, Becoming is transmuted into Being, a transmutation possessing a terrifying aspect, which Nietzsche would later discard. It is possible for a man to be so immersed in becoming that he loses the capacity to forget and consequently loses himself in its stream.[50] The repetition of events is treated as a possibility hinging on the accuracy of Pythagorean astronomy.

The Eternal Recurrence is a serious attempt to authenticate, and perhaps even deify, Becoming. Following in the steps of Heraclitus, Nietzsche proposed that Being, presumed to exist behind the mask of Becoming, is merely an illusion. If all is Becoming, it follows that, "the complex of causes will recur . . . it will create men again. . . . I shall return . . . not to a new life nor a similar life . . . [but] to this identical self-same life to teach once more the eternal recurrence of all things."[51] That Zarathustra is above all else the 'Teacher of the Eternal Recurrence' has been a stumbling block to those scholars who gladly would have consigned the doctrine to oblivion. Nevertheless, it is the Eternal Recurrence that transfers "the apparently vicious circle of dying and rising life into something divine" — the dying and rising Dionysius.[52]

The Eternal Recurrence solves the dilemma of the finite seeking the infinite by advocating the eternity of Becoming. In so doing, both the deceased God and nascent Nihilism are overcome and a higher era of history is inaugurated.[53] However, history in the strict sense is deprived of meaning. There is no goal, no real future. Only a voracious 'Now,' which prevents the world from lapsing into the absurd. *Circulos vitiosus deus.* As

---

49. Kaufmann, *Nietzsche,* 144-47; Nietzsche, *Untimely Meditations,* 120ff.

50. Nietzsche, *Untimely Meditations,* 62.

51. Nietzsche, *Zarathustra,* 237-38.

52. Laurence Lampert, *Leo Strauss and Nietzsche* (Chicago: Univ. of Chicago Press, 1996), 53.

53. Debra B. Bergoffen, "The Eternal Return Again." *International Studies in Philosophy* 15:2 (1983): 44.

Strauss indicates, "the Eternal Recurrence transforms the apparently vicious circle of dying and rising life into something divine . . . grounded on the insight that the world in its intelligible character is Will-to-Power and nothing else."[54]

Nietzsche spoke of this theory as 'the heaviest burden.' Faced with the horror of repeating one's life down to its most distressing particulars, he nevertheless found it possible to forgo cursing the 'demon' who so spoke and reply: "Thou art a God, and never did I hear anything so divine."[55] The Eternal Recurrence redeems the past by converting every 'It was' into 'I wanted it thus,' a heroic affirmation which is a magnificent tribute to life. Moreover, it is veritably a process of redemption: "*Amor fati:* let that henceforth be my love."[56] Necessity reigns! The 'yea-sayer' endorses the eternal whirl. Whatever is not actually in existence is dismissed. The postulation of any goal or end which is not actually in existence is a condemnation of existence. The future disappears. In a letter to Georg Brandes (1883), Nietzsche observed that the future has been 'extinguished' in him. A year later he described Zarathustra to Rhode as "a kind of abyss of the future."[57]

Since the Eternal Recurrence is the key to the transvaluation of values, it will be considered evil. This is the reason — as Strauss suggested to Lowith — that the doctrine had to be asserted *'Kampfhaft',* convulsively, "because he had to wean us and himself from the millennia-old pampering due to creation and providence."[58] Due to the influence of Christianity, the heroic, the exceptional, is fast disappearing. If the 'hard virtues' — those stigmatized as evil — are not resuscitated, the world will lapse into the gray on gray of the last men. Set free to develop, these 'terrible energies' will discard the tortured and deviant forms in which they have been imprisoned and begin to transform the world.

Nietzsche confirmed his place in the philosophy of history when his *Ecce Homo* was dated on the first day of the year One (September 30, 1888)

54. Lampert, *Strauss and Nietzsche,* 53, 55.

55. Nietzsche, *Joyful Wisdom,* no. 344, 270-71.

56. Nietzsche, *Joyful Wisdom,* no. 276, 213.

57. Leslie Chamberlain, *Nietzsche in Turin* (New York: Picador USA, 1997), 128.

58. Lampert, *Strauss and Nietzsche,* 109.

of the false chronology. In effect, this divides history into pre-Christian, Christian, and post-Christian segments, the latter inspired by the example of classical Greece. It appears that Nietzsche has mounted the treadmill of the eternal universe of the ancients. However, this impression may be deceptive. His recreation of antiquity is flawed, and his speculations contain undigested nuggets of theological leftovers and biblical attitudes, melded with Greek thought in the crucible of his imagination. The Eternal Recurrence, for example, bears a close resemblance to Origen's theory of *apocatastasis* in which everything is reduced to unity, the distinction between good and evil is obviated, and creation becomes an eternal act.[59] As Nietzsche attended Professor Steffenson's lectures on Origen,[60] some carryover is certainly possible. Origen's *apocatastasis,* with the individual replacing God, the shard of glass taking the place of the entire mirror, is not far removed from the Eternal Recurrence.

Nietzsche left an impressive *oeuvre.* His ideas attract or repel, defying indifference. They live and are not tailored to the expectations of those pedants he unkindly characterized as philosophical vermin.[61] To transform his insights into discursive language is not an easy task. Jaspers believed his thought was replete with self-contradictions, endless repetitions, and capriciousness,[62] and this is compounded by his use of disguise and masquerade. Yet, although Nietzsche's thought moves fleetingly like whitecaps on a choppy sea it nevertheless responds to currents which are fixed and deep. The interpreter's task is to chart these currents.

Predictably, his personality remains as hidden as the substance of his thought. Who was this man, surrounded by an incredibly strange atmosphere? What was he really like: a wanderer, the butt of childish pranks, a person who reminded an acquaintance of the Christ depicted by Murillo in 'The Feeding of the Five Thousand'?[63] Did he recognize himself in

---

59. Origen, *De princ.* 1,6,1; 3,5,3; 3,6,4-6. For a brief resume refer to Johannes Quasten, *Patrologia,* edicion espanol por Ignacio Onatibia (Madrid: BAC, 1961), 1:338-97.

60. *Conversations,* 95.

61. Frenzel, *Nietzsche,* 34.

62. Jaspers, *Nietzsche,* 10-11.

63. *Conversations,* 209.

Dostoyevsky's Underground Man, a work he found extraordinarily fascinating?[64] Is there ever more than furtive glimpses of the face behind the mask?

Nietzsche marks a watershed both in the philosophy of history and in the larger picture of European culture. His influence has been deep and pervasive: Yeats, Freud, Lawrence, Gide, Hartmann, Spengler, Mann, Conrad, Ortega, Scheler, Sartre, Weizmann, Shaw, and Foucault, and many others, are counted among those indebted to him, as are psychoanalysis, existentialism, and deconstructionism. His work has been used and abused, often by movements such as Hitler's National Socialism, with which he would have had little sympathy. In the philosophy of history his influence has been impressive, as his thought presents both a barrier to, and a point of departure for, further speculation. It must be rejected, followed, or circumvented. The options are limited: either return to the Christian eschatological tradition as do Soloviev and Berdyaev, build on certain Nietzschean insights, as do Spengler and Schmitt, or simply abandon the enterprise by proclaiming the end of history, a view popularized by Fukuyama and Niethammer.

Our thinker was scarcely one of those "exhausted hens" he ridiculed, whose eggs get smaller and smaller while their books get thicker and thicker.[65] The opposite is true. Each of his insights contains a wealth of possibilities often developing counter to his own vision. Nietzsche has a family resemblance to Balaam, from the land of Amaw (Numbers 24:13), whose destructive curses were transformed into a litany of blessings. Firmly convinced that European decline would continue and that nihilism would wring its civilization dry, he made a heroic, if faulty, effort to stem the tide. Bereft of religious faith if not of religious insight, Nietzsche became the unlikely portal through which philosophical speculation regarding history will be forced to pass for some time to come.

---

64. *Conversations,* 193.
65. Nietzsche, *Untimely Meditations,* 99.

CHAPTER 12

Through a Glass Darkly

While Friedrich Nietzsche was shedding his mortal coil under Frau
Förster-Nietzsche's care at Weimar, he was rapidly becoming a celebrity. This was primarily due to the efforts of his sister, who became the
caretaker of his work, even adding to it by arbitrarily piecing together
fragments to compose *The Will to Power* and, in so doing, foisting upon
him much of her Pan-Germanic ideology. She became an admirer of Hitler and succeeded in making the cult of Nietzsche equal, if not superior,
to the Wagner cult at Bayreuth, presided over by Nietzsche's 'Ariadne',
Cosima Wagner.

The Nietzsche cult burgeoned. Richard Strauss's tone poem, *Also
Sprach Zarathustra,* premiered in Frankfurt in 1896. Gustav Mahler completed his *Third Symphony,* originally entitled *The Gay Science,* the same
year. Later, George Bernard Shaw's *Man and Superman,* a popularized
version of Nietzsche's thought, appeared in London. Interest in the philosopher was to cross the Atlantic. H. L. Mencken dedicated a surprisingly mediocre study to his work, though he did produce a superior translation of *The Antichrist.* Overall, Nietzsche was influential in turning the
general mood away from the optimism of the *fin-de-siècle* towards the
pessimism characteristic of the twentieth century.

While the nineteenth century produced several utopias, the twentieth
veered in the opposite direction. Two works that illustrated this turnabout
were Karl Kraus's *The Last Days of Mankind* and Oswald Spengler's *De-*

cline of the West, works that breathed decadence, collapse, and decay.[1] As Josef Pieper indicated, the extreme pessimism of the age should be regarded as a symptom of the decay of the Enlightenment doctrine of progress.[2]

The Decline of the West was published in July 1918, precisely at the turning point of the Great War (World War I). It is composed of two volumes, the first subtitled "Form and Reality," the second "World-historical Perspectives." Spengler claims to present a new outlook on history and the philosophy of history. While acknowledging his debt to Goethe and Nietzsche he takes Nietzsche to task as a romantic who fears to look reality in the face and dismisses the Overman as a "castle in the air." In the wings stands "the great Joachim": "the first thinker of the Hegelian stamp who shattered the dualistic world-form of Augustine, and with his essentially Gothic intellect stated the new Christianity of his time."[3]

The book elicited much attention and commentary. Schroeter's *Der Streit um Spengler* records a list of some three hundred critics.[4] The academic establishment was, on the whole, cool. Adolf von Harnack wrote Spengler that he found the book dubious, arbitrary, and unproven.[5] Using analogy as his interpretive tool, Spengler attempted to predetermine history by following the "still untraveled stages" in Western European-American culture, which is presently in the process of fulfillment.[6] He provided a wealth of observations, analyses, and speculations imbedded in a veritable mosaic of historical data. Nevertheless, this abundance does not suffice to identify Spengler with the philosopher he invokes "who will tell us in what language history is written and how it is to be read."[7]

The core of Spengler's thought is found in speculations on culture

1. Refer to Arthur Herman, *The Idea of Decline in Western History* (New York: Free Press, 1997), 224-25; Russell Jacoby, *The End of Utopia* (New York: Basic Books, 1999), 155f.

2. Josef Pieper, *The End of Time: A Meditation on the Philosophy of History,* trans. Michael Bullock (New York: Pantheon, 1954), 77.

3. Oswald Spengler, *The Decline of the West,* trans. Charles Francis Atkinson (New York: Alfred A. Knopf, 1939), 1:xiv, 19-20.

4. Atkinson in Spengler, *Decline,* 1:x.

5. Oswald Spengler, *Selected Letters 1913-1936,* trans. Arthur Helps (New York: Alfred A. Knopf, 1966), 85-86.

6. Spengler, *Decline,* 1:3.

7. Spengler, *Decline,* 1:8.

conceived as a human organism with its own distinct personality and style. It is the point at which man lifts himself above nature; the soul which has arrived at self-expression through the medium of sensible forms. Each culture has its own possibilities that arise, ripen, decay, and do not return. This takes place, we are told, with the superb aimlessness of the flowers of the field, without direction from God or Demiurge. Thucydides represents the classical man who lives in the pure present. This is the outlook of the mature statesman. Yet Thucydides lacked perspective, that ability to survey the history of cultures. This is the privilege of modern man. Classical mathematics conceives of things as they are, as present, timeless magnitudes. Modern mathematics, on the contrary, conceives of things as they become, as functions.[8] The classical was the culture of the small. The Greeks possessed no word for space. Modernity liberated geometry from the visual, algebra from magnitude and united both in function theory. It is the culture of the infinite.[9]

Moreover, the difference between classical and modern is reflected in their respective views of history. Spengler maintains that the Ptolemaic system, in which cultures are made to follow orbits around ourselves at the center, be jettisoned in favor of the Copernican system which allows of no privileged position:

> I see, in place of that empty figment of one linear history . . . the drama of a number of mighty cultures . . . each stamping its material, its mankind, in its own image: each having its own idea, its own passions, its own life, will and feeling, its own death.[10]

Civilization is the finale, the tail end, of a culture, its strict and necessary outcome, its inevitable destiny.[11] This transition from culture to civilization took place in the classical world in the fourth century BC and in the modern world in the nineteenth. The hallmark of civilization is money, or rather, the money-spirit. Skepticism is its intellectual expres-

8. Spengler, *Decline,* 1:14-15.
9. Spengler, *Decline,* 1:75, 77-78, 86-87.
10. Spengler, *Decline,* 1:18ff.
11. Spengler, *Decline,* 1:31.

sion. Sounding very much like a Marxist-Leninist, Spengler affirms that imperialism is civilization unadulterated.[12]

Culture and civilization differ radically. The culture-man is inner-directed. The civilization-man is outer-directed. Taking this distinction into account it is evident that the history of the West is not an unlimited ascending movement but rather a limited segment of at best a few centuries. It has the advantage that it can be calculated from available precedent. History can no longer be thought of in accordance with the linear theory fashioned during the Enlightenment. History is the story of the rise and fall of cultures, not of progress and continuity.

Spengler distinguishes between the Apollinian, the Magian, and the Faustian Cultures. The Apollinian is the classical; the Magian includes the Arabic, Judaic, and Byzantine; the Faustian is the modern European with its powerful appetite for the erasure of limits.[13] Each culture possesses its own unique image of the soul. The classical is best represented by Plato's *Phaedrus:* chariot with *nous* (mind) as the charioteer. The Magian is reflected in a strict dualism, such as those found in the Gnostics and Neoplatonists. The Faustian, eminently dynamic and historical, centers on the will. The world-as-cavern (Magian) differs as much from the world-as-extension (Faustian) as it does from the Apollinian world as the sum of corporeal things.[14]

Spengler maintains that a genuinely Faustian treatment of history has been lacking. A *prise de distance* is required, a mental detachment that is able to view the 'fact of man' from a distance and "regard the individual cultures, one's own included, as one regards the range of mountain peaks along a horizon."[15] The classical man is totally inserted in the present. The modern man has an eye both to past and future. As the picture of history is fundamentally a memory-picture, it is the privileged domain of modernity. It is closed to classical man, who, strictly speaking, has no memory and hence no history.[16]

---

12. Spengler, *Decline,* 1:34-35; 45-46.
13. Spengler, *Decline,* 1:183ff., 335.
14. Spengler, *Decline,* 1:304ff.; 2:233.
15. Spengler, *Decline,* 1:93-94.
16. Spengler, *Decline,* 1:97, 103.

It is the great cultures that provide access to the 'inner form' of history as they constitute a collective biography. Spengler uses two traditional metaphors to make his point. Every culture passes through stages that can be compared to the ages of man or the seasons of the year.[17] At its inception a culture is austere, controlled, intense, infused with life-force. In summer, this consciousness spreads from the ruling class to the population at large. By autumn, the progressive weakening of forms leads to the exhaustion of culture and the beginnings of civilization. In winter, civilization, a parasite that clings to the decayed roots of culture, reaches its maturity.[18] In European culture, the winter stage began in the nineteenth century.

Individuals — historically-relevant individuals — recapitulate the stages of the culture to which they belong, a point that was being made by Freud vis-à-vis the instinctual life: ontogeny recapitulates phylogeny. Each culture possesses a destiny idea. Spengler points to Oedipus and King Lear as representing the classical and modern cultures. There also are subsidiary ideas. For example, the idea of the French Revolution is the victory of the inorganic megalopolis over the organic countryside. This historical event produced the transition from culture to civilization.[19]

Spengler's opinion of the man of civilization is unsparing. He is without tradition or religion, scrap material who obtains mechanistically what his forefathers, the creators of culture, had lived organically. He views these men *en bloc,* as the inorganic, cosmopolitan masses of the megalopolis, lapsing into non-history. Masses who, prodded by resentment, persecute every sort of form, structure, order, and hierarchy.

The world-as-history and the world-as-nature travel together down the same path until the baroque era when, for the first time, they were separated. This is due to the modern Faustian infinity-craving, which reduces human history into a mere episode of world history and the earth into a minor star lost among millions of solar systems.[20] Even within human history man can be said to be without history both before the birth of

17. Spengler, *Decline,* 1:107.
18. This paraphrase of Spengler is taken from Herman, *Idea of Decline,* 238-39.
19. Spengler, *Decline,* 1:148.
20. Spengler, *Decline,* 2:28.

a culture and after its death when civilization has attained its definite form.[21] Primary urges grow and enter into conflict when culture reaches its maturity, ultimately taking the form of an incessant struggle between Money and Law.

Spengler believed the age in which he lived was transitional, "between the late-culture period with its mature forms and the age of great individuals in a formless world."[22] A period of "gigantic conflicts" is arriving, one that would move Europe from "Napoleonism" to "Caesarism," from authoritarianism to tyranny. The way for Caesarism has been prepared by the "megalopolitan masses" who have demolished traditional forms. And Caesarism is a fall into primitivism, a return to formlessness.[23]

Nationalism and democracy are in the last stages of decay. Spengler was not alone in predicting that race was destined to become the most important factor since all ideals will succumb to its lure. Money is the villain of the piece. It not only destroys intellect but inveigles democracy to be its own executioner. The struggle between democracy and Caesarism, between the last stage of civilization and the fall into non-history, comes down to the struggle between economics and politics, a struggle that will see the latter emerge as the victor.[24] Though Caesarism grows on the soil of democracy its roots plunge downward to the underground of blood — of race. *The Decline of the West* ends on a note of warning: "This moment . . . the moment when money is celebrating its last victories . . . the Caesarism that is to succeed approaches with quiet, firm steps."[25]

Caught between anarchy and what he called "soulless Americanism," convinced that in late civilization even the most convincing idea is only the mask of zoological striving,[26] Spengler tilted in the direction of Hitler's NSDAP. His apology for Germany's move to the right, Prussianism and Socialism, appeared in 1920. He was awarded the Nietzsche prize, but his enthusiasm cooled. After meeting Hitler at the Bayreuth Festival

21. Spengler, *Decline,* 2:48.
22. Spengler, *Decline,* 2:415-16.
23. Spengler, *Decline,* 2:431.
24. Spengler, *Decline,* 2:463-65.
25. Spengler, *Decline,* 2:507.
26. Spengler, *Selected Letters,* 31.

(1933), he published *The Hour of Decision,* which was promptly banned. Though his early advocacy might have paved the way for what was to come, it should be evident that his sights were focused in another direction, upon the horrors of a civilization which had become a machine and the "oozing flood of commercialism" it would bring in its wake.[27]

Spengler's notions of culture and civilization and their interrelation, together with his surgical dissection of contemporary civilization and its deplorable outgrowths, are valid contributions to the philosophy of history. His predictions were on target, albeit woefully short-term. The nonhistoric age in which money power would be defeated might conceivably, if mistakenly, include the Hitler and Stalin regimes. At this point his prescience stalls — for although there is a death of each culture, there seems to be no end to their succession, which, in Faustian fashion, moves towards the infinite. Lacking Nietzsche's gymnastic ability to reify becoming without a goal or end, the process is emptied of meaning. The "superb aimlessness" that is invoked is perhaps no more than another mask on the face of Nothing.

Carl Schmitt, like Spengler, succumbed to the lure of the NSDAP, albeit provisionally, which brought him obscurity after World War II. This was in direct contrast to the celebrity he enjoyed during the Weimar years, which rested on such works as *Political Theology* (1922), *The Crisis of Parliamentary Democracy* (1923), and *Political Romanticism* (1925). Almost a half-century later his works became the object of an extensive, albeit often hostile, commentary. After his death in April 1985, three months shy of his ninety-seventh birthday, he has enjoyed a Renaissance of sorts, with many of his works translated into English and other languages. Although several of his theories will be mentioned, it is a relatively unheralded work, *Land and Sea,* which will mark the nodal point of the present study. Published in 1942, only a few copies passed out of Germany, the great bulk of the edition stored in the publisher's warehouse.[28]

Born into a devout Catholic family in 1888, Schmitt was marked for

27. Cited in Herman, *Idea of Decline,* 229.

28. Carl Schmitt, *Tierra y Mar (Land und Meer),* trad. de Rafael Fernandez-Quintanilla (Madrid: Instituto de Estudios Politicos, 1952), i.

the priesthood but opted for the study of law, receiving his doctorate from Strasbourg in 1910. His initial ultramontane sympathies became muted after World War I when he fell under the influence of Hobbes and moved towards *Realpolitik,* appropriating his dictum that "autoritas, non veritas, facit legem."[29] After attempting to prop up the crumbling Weimar Republic, Schmitt participated in the National Socialist Regime from 1933 to 1936, voicing opinions that were considered to be anti-Semitic. After being attacked by the *Schwarze Korps,* an official publication of the SS, he retired from active politics and remained in semi-retirement until after the termination of the war.

Schmitt's mind was a veritable crucible of ideas, some original and perceptive, others tarted-up chestnuts. Among the most important are those of the "total state," the "friend-enemy criterion" of politics, the "legal world revolution," the "political," the "primacy of decision," and the theory of "equal chance" aimed at excluding extreme movements from the political arena. Perhaps the most important, his notion of the "exception," both confirms the rule and manifests its existence. Schmitt followed Hobbes in his realistic appraisal of mankind and his unitary conception of sovereignty, and Donoso Cortés in his reduction of the discourse of statecraft to the theological. Not surprisingly, he considered Hobbes's *Leviathan* and de Maistre's *Du Pape* the most important works produced by modernity.[30]

He came to realize that the history of the past few centuries could not be understood without insight into the process of secularization. Accordingly he traced its growth from the theological stage by way of the metaphysical to the ethical and economic.[31] This provided a gateway for two of his most important theories, that of the "exception" and that of the "political." The first is important because it is the sovereign who decides on the exception, any severe disturbance that requires extraordinary measures:

29. Carl Schmitt, *Political Theology,* trans. George Schwab (Cambridge: MIT Press, 1985), xi-xiii. Cf. George Bendersky, *Carl Schmitt: Theorist for the Reich* (Princeton: Princeton Univ. Press, 1983).

30. Heinrich Meier, *The Lesson of Carl Schmitt,* trans. Marcus Brainerd (Chicago: Univ. of Chicago Press, 1998), 130n.20.

31. Schmitt, *Political Theology,* preface to second edition, 2.

"In the exception the power of real life breaks through the crust of a mechanism that has become torpid by repetition."[32]

The "political" is the bellwether of social reality. It is the total. A political decision precedes every constitution and provides the basis for the legal system. It protects mankind against the wiles of the Antichrist, a figure which enthralled and terrified Schmitt. He believed that a world sunk in apathetic contentment, not unlike Nietzsche's "last men," is the harbinger of the apocalyptic world-state that will proceed to devour everything. He considered the rejection of enmity among men to be the most evident sign of the advancing monolith. Schmitt noted in 1947 that the distinction between friend and enemy as well as the fact that enmity perdures among men appalled most people.[33]

The "political" has three major foes: political romanticism, which avoids the either/or of decision by taking refuge in eternal chatter; anarchism, which paralyzes decision in paradisaical this-worldliness; economic-technological thinking, which is incapable of even conceiving a political idea.[34] Schmitt insisted on maintaining the dignity of the state against the pluralism of economic interest. As he maintained that the bourgeoisie legal state is the expression of a decision for the nonpolitical, he endorsed a struggle against liberal democracy and the overpowering "religion of technicity."

The utopian fantasy of One World is unmasked as a plot to accelerate the reign of Antichrist, a world in which history comes to an end. To account for the respites allotted to humanity, which delays the advent of the End Time, Schmitt adopted St. Paul's notion of the *Katechon* (2 Thess. 2:7), a force which restrains the Evil One.[35] He believed that there has been an uninterrupted succession of "restrainers," among whom he included the Roman Empire, the Jesuits, and Emperor Franz Joseph. By

32. Schmitt, *Political Theology*, 5, 5n.1, 15.

33. Meier, *Lesson of Carl Schmitt*, 135n.35.

34. Schmitt, *Political Theology*, 55-56; Carl Schmitt, *Political Romanticism*, trans. Guy Oakes (Cambridge: MIT Press, 1985), 162 et al.

35. The notion of *Katchon* can be found in both early and late works of Schmitt. See *Theodor Daubler's "Nordlicht"* (Berlin: Duncker and Humblot, 1974 [1916]), and *Der Nomos der Erde* (Berlin: Duncker and Humblot, 1974).

preventing the establishment of a World-State they held in check the coming of the Antichrist.

All of Schmitt's speculations revolve around his conception of Christianity. He disagreed vehemently with Lowith's view that the New Testament is above all else a call to repentance. Christianity, he urges, is not a morality, a doctrine, or a religion in the sense of comparative religious studies, but a historical event of infinite uniqueness.[36] A case may be made, taking liberty with Schmitt's vocabulary, that Christianity is the "exception" that validates not only itself but everything else as it rests on the sovereignty of God. His struggle in favor of the political is a struggle concerning the interpretation of history.

Land and Sea provides a novel interpretation of history, which also goes back to a venerable theory that Schmitt believed to be Kabbalistic, attributing it to Isaac Abravanel (1437-1508). He seems to have believed that it uncovered a secret Jewish agenda not much different from that presented in later anti-Semitic literature such as *The Rabbi's Speech* and *The Protocols of the Elders of Zion*.[37] The ancient theme, of which it is a variation, reads as follows: at the end of the present era, Behemoth, the land monster, and Leviathan, the sea monster, will challenge God and be roundly defeated. The final banquet then takes place with their carcasses served as food.

Schmitt's version shifts the struggle to the monsters: Behemoth and Leviathan slaughter each other in the presence of the Jewish people. After the battle they take the skins of the monsters, construct beautiful pavilions, and celebrate a solemn banquet with their flesh.[38] The difference is obvious, as is the message. Actually, the Kabbalistic views that filtered into scholarly discourse were usually more profound and far more complex. Nachmanides is a good example. His interpretation of the book of Daniel computes that 1,290 years will pass between the destruction of the Temple and the defeat of the Abomination. According to his calculations, grounded principally on *gematria* (number mysticism), redemptive activity will begin

36. Carl Schmitt, *Roman Catholicism and Political Form,* trans. G. L. Ulmen (Westport, Conn.: Greenwood Press, 1996).

37. These classical tracts were taken from Goedsche's novel *Biarritz* and Joly's *Dialogue aux Enfers entre Montesquieu et Machiavel.*

38. Schmitt, *Tierra y Mar,* 111.

in 1358, the Messianic era will end in 1403, to be followed by the world to come.[39] This is only a necessarily truncated example of a rich literature.

The principal interpretation encountered in *Land and Sea,* though presented in haphazard manner and sandwiched between lengthy segments of extraneous material, is a novel reading of the "ancient theory" that history is basically a journey through the four elements: earth, air, fire, and water, not necessarily in that order.[40] Man is a terrestrial being, water the mysterious origin of life. Land people and sea people have different notions of time and space. But man is not absorbed by his environment. He is able to choose the element to bring about a new total form of historic existence by organizing himself as a function of the chosen element.[41]

For millennia the earth held center stage. Naval warfare was simply land warfare on ships. The battle of Lepanto (1571) — the great victory of the Spanish and Venetian fleets over Islam — was the last of this type. It was fought in the same manner as was the battle of Actium (31 BC), which took place in approximately the same area. The Age of Discovery initiated a revolution in marine technology. The Dutch invented more types of ships than all other nations combined. Later, the English succeeded in creating a maritime world empire. This transferred the center of existence from earth to water. A "spatial revolution" was effected.[42]

Space is important to Schmitt. The different sciences have fashioned their own concepts of space. But history does not wait for the sciences. Every time new bodies of land or sea are added to the collective consciousness space is transformed, a spatial revolution occurs, which ineluctably accompanies great historic transformations.[43] The expression *Novus Orbis,* found in Seneca's *Medea,* was, after 1492, applied to the newly discovered America.

The first spatial revolution, strictly speaking, took place in the sixteenth and seventeenth centuries.[44] From Copernicus's *De Revolutionibus*

39. Nachmanides, *El libre de la Redempcio i Altres Escrits,* trad. Eduard Feliu I Mabres (Barcelona: U. de Barcelona, 1933).

40. Schmitt, *Tierra y Mar,* 111.

41. Schmitt, *Tierra y Mar,* 11, 15.

42. Schmitt, *Tierra y Mar,* 55-56.

43. Schmitt, *Tierra y Mar,* 58.

44. Schmitt, *Tierra y Mar,* 66f.

orbium onward there is an advance towards the idea of infinite empty space. This new spatial concept was duly reflected in the art of the epoch: painting, architecture, and music. For Schmitt every fundamental ordering is spatial: "Every change or notable variation of the image of the earth goes united with political change, with a new distribution of the goal, a new conquest of territories."[45] The division of the world in 1493 by Pope Alexander VI signaled the beginning of a new *nomos* of the Earth. The Industrial Revolution transformed the Leviathan from a great fish into a great machine.[46]

It seems that the machine is the latest port of call for the chameleon-like notion of progress, which is closely bound to the inorganic, cosmopolitan phenomenon of the masses. Progress originally rested on a religious scaffolding. This was jettisoned and progress then rested on human autonomy in a desacralized world. It still harbored a purpose, a goal. Now, it is entering a stage which some have called "technopoly,"[47] in which progress loses purpose while requiring the submission of all forms of cultural life to the dictatorship of technology. This is the extreme expression of the loss of history.

Of the pages dedicated to the principal theme, the majority are dedicated to the interaction between land and sea. Future possibilities are discussed only summarily. Schmitt indicates that with the appearance of the airplane a new spatial dimension is brought into play. A third element is in the process of being conquered and used as an instrument of the human will to provoke a new crisis in the history of the West.[48] This element he first considered to be air, suggesting that a giant bird should be added to Behemoth and Leviathan. However, if the combustion engine is taken into account as well as the technology by which man exercises his dominion of the air, perhaps fire instead of air will be the next element.[49]

The imperium of millennia enjoyed by earth and water is fading to-

45. Schmitt, *Tierra y Mar,* 74.

46. Schmitt, *Tierra y Mar,* 103.

47. Cf. Neil Postman, *Technopoly: The Surrender of Culture to Technology* (New York: Vintage, 1993).

48. Schmitt, *Tierra y Mar,* iv.

49. Schmitt, *Tierra y Mar,* 110-11.

gether with its norms and traditions. The future *nomos* is approaching on the horizon. To some it represents death and destruction, to others the end of the world. But what is to come, urges Schmitt, is neither chaos nor pure nothing:

Auch hier sind Götter und Welten
Gross ist ihr Mass.

Unlike Spengler, Schmitt did not euchre himself into a dead end. He melded his speculations on secular history with the End Times depicted in the Apocalypse. History takes on the character of a holding action, of restraining the building of a World-State, the window by which the Antichrist enters to claim his domain. The secular movement of history is connected to its apocalyptic denouement by means of the notion of the political.

The progression of the four elements as marking historical stages or epochs is an engaging conception that unfortunately is left unfinished and unarticulated. The secular and religious form an uneasy alliance. The next chapter will study the turn to a religious view of history as expressed by Russian thinkers annealed in Orthodoxy; the Postscript steps into the void of non-history as presented by the 'End of History' thinkers.

CHAPTER 13

Embers: Soloviev and Berdyaev

R ussia and Spain are by far the most enigmatic of European nations: the infinite expanse where the continent ends and the great bull hide with which it begins. José Ortega y Gasset once referred to Spain as a Western Tibet.[1] The same can be said, with perhaps more justification, of Russia. The sense of the alien and foreign, of otherness, subsists in both into the twenty-first century. Religion, or its secular analogue, ideology, holds a commanding position. In both, the concrete is favored over the abstract, the private over the public.

Differences abound. The Russian mother-earth syndrome is absent in Spain as is communal stress reflected in *Sobornost* and the quirky asceticism of *Yurodstvo,* being the fool for the sake of God. Russia, for its part, is free of that peculiarly Spanish type of egotism *(Yo-ismo)* and the multicolored spectacle of the bullring. Theologically, the Russian tilts towards immanence, the Spaniard towards transcendence. Politically, the directions are reversed. Don Quixote tilts at windmills because he knows full well that they are giants. Ivan Karamazov's catalogue of horrors demands immediate solution from a higher authority.

Philosophy has not been the forte of either Spain or Russia, at least in the modern era. In Spain, philosophy reached its zenith in the Middle

1. Cited by J. N. Hillgarth, *The Spanish Kingdoms [1250-1517]* (Oxford: Clarendon Press, 1978), 2:625n.3.

Ages and notably diminished after 1492, with its place taken by theology and spirituality. Philosophy was a latecomer in Russia. Even theology did not exist in Russian Orthodoxy for a lengthy period when the tradition of Platonism and Greek patristics had been forgotten.[2] On the popular level we encounter a motley crew of pilgrims, *starets,* ecstatics, and fringe persons who have at least a family resemblance to the *picaros,* students, religious, and pseudo-religious of the Spanish scene. Spanish monarchs such as Isabella and Philip II, though personally religious, were primarily secular in their political aspirations. Russian rulers, from Ivan the Terrible to atheists such as Lenin and Stalin, retain a millenarian cast.

Two readings of a popular myth may serve to clarify the situation. The invisible city of Kitezh, in the original Russian version, is an ideal situated beyond space and time. Hidden by God and protected by his hand, the city will again become visible only when Christ returns. Unamuno's variation on the theme has a sunken city — the past and its ideals — which surfaces now and again in the mind of the protagonist only to sink into the depths. The Russian Kitezh is detached from the present, a utopia situated on a distant horizon. The Spanish, though never entirely recoverable, continues to inform the present.

Spain and Russia have been obsessed by the eschatological. The surrealistic portraits of Beatus of Liebana were, centuries later, provided with a discursive carapace by Donoso Cortés. In Russia perhaps the closest analogue to Donoso would be Vladimir Soloviev, a rather bizarre combination of philosopher, theologian, and theosophist, a man who was convinced that he had been favored with three visions of *Sophia* or Wisdom, identified alternately with the world-soul and with spiritualized humanity. They are duly recorded in his "Three Meetings."[3]

As a child Vladimir Soloviev (1853-1900) was something of a prodigy — pious, self-confessedly odd, given to strange dreams. After an adolescent bout of atheism he returned to religious faith by way of Spinoza, from whose works he acquired a profound sense of God's reality and of

2. Nicolai Berdyaev, *The Russian Idea,* trans. R. M. French (Hudson, N.Y.: Lindisfarne Press, 1992), 173.

3. Vladimir Soloviev, *Lectures on Divine Humanity,* trans. Peter Zouboff, ed. Boris Jakin (Hudson, N.Y.: Lindisfarne Press, 1995), xiii-xiv.

the unity of the world, two characteristics that would distinguish his work. What could be called his seminal work, *Lectures on Divine Humanity,* were given as a series of lectures at St. Petersburg (1878-1881) and attracted a noteworthy audience, including Dostoyevsky and Tolstoy. However, a lecture in which he opposed capital punishment brought about his expulsion from the university.

A man of many talents, he excelled in literary criticism, translated Plato and Kant, and wrote light verse. He attacked the xenophobic anti-Semitism of the later Slavophiles and his strong Roman Catholic sympathies led to the censorship of several of his books. When he turned to the task of reuniting the Christian churches, he became something of a wanderer and took up ascetical practices with an eye on his utopian project of a future theocracy — spiritual authority falling to the Pope and temporal authority to the Tsar. Several works were published, including *The Meaning of Love* (1897), *The Justification of the Good* (1892-1894), and *Three Conversations Concerning War, Progress, and the End of History* (1900). He died on July 31, 1900, at forty-seven years of age.

Soloviev was a man, as Berdyaev remarked, who, in his own person, united mysticism and philosophy.[4] With the zeal of a Neoplatonist he was obsessed by the reality of unity. As a Christian he maintained that the world, due to the Incarnation, had become energized by humanity. It has become a factor in the life of God and is advancing toward total unity. In the intellectual world, he called for a synthesis of science, philosophy, and religion to restore its unity. Basically, this is Soloviev's version of the advent of the Kingdom of God on earth to be accomplished by the free union of humanity and the world with the Absolute Principle — God.[5]

In this process of unification the Christian East and West should both participate. The West attempted to base a universal culture on humanity alone while the East, though it preserved a 'divine element', failed to embody it in a culture. Soloviev suggests that the divine element preserved

4. *Vekhi (Landmarks),* trans. Marshall S. Shatz and Judith E. Zimmerman (Armonk, N.Y.: M. E. Sharpe, 1994), 14.

5. Soloviev, *Lectures,* ix.

by the East can be actualized by the human element developed by the West:

> Only after the human principle has completely isolated itself and come to know its helplessness in this isolation, can it enter into a free union with the divine foundation of Christianity preserved in the Eastern Church, and as a result of free union, give birth to a spiritual humankind.[6]

The Body of Christ, by the end of time, will increase to encompass all of humanity and all of nature into a single divine-human organism, what Soloviev calls *Bogochelovechestvo*.

Energized by religion, everything moves towards this goal, "the connection of humanity and the world with the Absolute Principle and the focus of all that exists."[7] This movement towards unity also has its practical consequences: it is required to transmute human deeds from meaningless phenomena into meaningful events. The contemporary world reduces religion to a "pitiful thing" hidden in a corner of the inner world when it attempts to organize humanity without God. The failed attempts of the French Revolution and its socialist sequelae to do so, to build society on a secular basis, indicate that religion, which confesses the reality of God, is a prime necessity.[8]

Soloviev aspired, like all utopians, to constitute a 'New World'. To accomplish this he insisted that the Kingdom of the World be made subservient to the Kingdom of God, and this he thought could be effected by the church spiritualizing society, by making society its instrument. But to do this in such a way that the subordination be voluntary and harmonious, the human person has to be given his due importance. When belief in God, divine in actuality, and belief in the human person, divine in possibility, are actualized in full, they then "meet in the one, complete, integral truth of Divine Humanity."[9]

6. Soloviev, *Lectures,* 174.
7. Soloviev, *Lectures,* 1, 10.
8. Soloviev, *Lectures,* xiii-xiv.
9. Soloviev, *Lectures,* 23-24.

This cosmic process has three principal aspects or stages: (1) the becoming of nature, which issues in man; (2) the becoming of history, which issues in Christ; (3) the becoming of the church, which issues in the Kingdom of God.[10] Religion proceeds from one root and develops by stages into different types. The Divine Principle is first recognized in the forces of nature — polytheism. When nature loses its divine status, a negative type, exemplified by Buddhism and Platonism, arises. With the Mosaic Law, Divinity is revealed as a 'willing person' and Christianity as the new divine-human covenant that "restores all humankind, and through humankind, also the whole of nature."[11]

The Jewish principle (the unity of God) is supplemented by the Christian principle (personal incarnation). In this way, humanity acts as the bridge uniting the divine to the natural. The ultimate goal of the Divine is the deification *(theosis)* of simply everything "by giving all that exists the form of an absolute organism."[12] The Incarnation connects God to man and to the history of the world. Tilting to the heterodox, Soloviev contends that the Incarnation of Jesus Christ was only the final link of a long series of anticipatory incarnations by which humanity moves towards Divine-Humanity.[13]

Berdyaev pointed out that there is a sense in which Soloviev's thought is a philosophy of history inasmuch as it is the account of the movement of humanity towards God-Manhood, the all-embracing Unity.[14] This reflects the ongoing creation of the world and announces its cosmic transfiguration. Soloviev did interpret history in this way — the pilgrimage of man from his primitive origin to a cosmic apotheosis — until disillusion set in, provoked by the problem of evil. This interpretation is indebted to Neoplatonism, Spinoza, and Hegel, strands that meld with a Russian na-

---

10. George L. Kline, "Russian Religious Thought," in *Nineteenth Century Religious Thought in the West,* ed. Ninian Smart, John Clayton, Stephen T. Katz, and Patrick Sherry (Cambridge: Cambridge Univ. Press, 1985), 2:212. Cf. Hans Urs von Balthasar, *Herrlichkeit: Eine theologische Aesthetik,* 2 vols. (Einsiedeln, Switzerland, 1962).

11. Soloviev, *Lectures,* 71.

12. Soloviev, *Lectures,* 137.

13. Soloviev, *Lectures,* 157.

14. Berdyaev, *Russian Idea,* 187.

tional idea grounded in religio-cultural messianism. As Bulgakov stated, "the outstanding spokesmen of our national self-consciousness, Dostoevski, the Slavophiles and Soloviev linked it with the world mission of the Russian Church or Russian culture."[15]

Soloviev was not an admirer of Western thought. He classified the entire period from John Scotus Erigena (ninth century) to his day as "positivism." However, apart from his preference for Plato, he was indebted to Western thinkers such as Spinoza and Hegel and had a high opinion of Schopenhauer and Eduard von Hartmann, whose Philosophy of the Unconscious impressed him greatly, chiefly because of two propositions he encountered there. First, the recognition of the concrete, unitary Spirit as the Absolute Principle. Second, assurance that the supreme goal is achieved by a purposeful movement of cosmic development.

He believed that von Hartmann had marked the high point, the ultimate outcome, of Western thought. It is only one step to maintaining, as Soloviev did, that the truths affirmed by philosophy in the form of rational knowledge were identical to those affirmed in the form of faith by the Christian East.[16] Moreover, as he believed that philosophy had its beginning when the individual separated his thought from the common faith, this process also serves to heal the breach between faith and reason which had been initiated by philosophy.

The striving for unity endows time with meaning. Through time, history winds laboriously towards its consummation in God-Manhood. But, when Soloviev broaches the matter directly, in *War, Progress, and the End of History*, this solution falters. Here the question of evil is encountered in all of its radicality. Is evil merely a natural defect that will vanish with the growth of good? Or is it a power requiring assistance from 'another sphere' for successful combat?[17] As the latter option appears to win the argument this shuts the door on melioristic utopias. Chadayev had already complained, over fifty years previously, to Schelling that Hegelianism was

15. Sergei Bulgakov, "Heroism and Asceticism." *Vekhi*, p. 44.

16. Vladimir Soloviev, *The Crisis of Western Philosophy*, trans. and ed. Boris Jakim (Hudson, N.Y.: Lindisfarne Press, 1996), 148-49.

17. Vladimir Soloviev, *War, Progress, and the End of History*, trans. Alexander Bakshy, (London: Univ. of London Press, 1915), xix.

being used by Russian nationalists to create a retrospective utopia which involved an arrogant apotheosis of the Russian people.[18]

The principal characters of *War, Progress, and the End of History* are Mr. Z, Soloviev's alter ego, and 'the Prince', who acts as his Tolstoyian counterpoise. Mr. Z's views run against the prevailing public orthodoxy of the day. War is not an absolute evil. Peace is not an absolute good. To the view that all men have a deposit of good and can be reformed he replies: "Why didn't Christ use the power of his spirit to awaken the good hidden in the souls of Judas and Herod?" To the optimistic belief that European culture will beneficently permeate the world, Mr. Z observes that progress is unfailingly a symptom of the End Times. Why this turnabout? He was convinced that the good peace brought by Christ had been replaced by the bad peace which endeavors to unite antithetical elements — "the world-unifying power of the Antichrist who will . . . cast a glittering veil of good and truth over the mystery of utter lawlessness."[19]

Social panaceas are dismissed. Tolstoyian nonresistance to evil is rejected. Evil is a noxious presence, one reflected by death, more powerful than transient life. The only solution is resurrection: "the Kingdom of God is the Kingdom of Life triumphing through resurrection."[20] This solution is given an apocalyptic counterpoint in "The Short Story of Antichrist," written ostensibly by a school friend of Mr. Z, the monk Pansophius.

In the story, a United States of Europe is established after an occupation by Mongols lasting fifty years. Europe is in a sad state. Both materialism and naive faith are at a low ebb. A man who is a believer, who possesses splendid qualities, but loves only himself, becomes convinced that he is the savior, the definitive savior of humanity: "Christ . . . was a reformer of mankind, whereas I am called to be the benefactor."[21] Instead of separating men by means of the criterion of good and evil, he will unite them through benefit and profit. When, in a rare moment, he becomes aware that Christ may well be the true savior, he is bombarded by a pleth-

18. Kline, "Russian Religious Thought," 181-82.
19. Soloviev, *War, Progress,* xxxii.
20. Soloviev, *War, Progress,* 165.
21. Soloviev, *War, Progress,* 189.

ora of violent emotions. Fear passes into envy, envy into hatred, which produces a fall into despair. He attempts suicide. Satan then appears and claims him as his son.[22]

In the meantime, the pretender's *The Open Way to Universal Peace and Well-Being* is everywhere accepted as authentic revelation. With the aid of Apollonius, a Catholic Bishop-Magician, he gains the plaudits of the world by obtaining universal peace and complete equality, abolishing hunger, and providing unflagging entertainment.[23] Elected President of Europe, then Emperor, he moves his residence to Jerusalem and builds — shades of Hitler's projected Berlin monstrosity — an Empire Temple dedicated to the union of all religious cults. Each branch of Christianity is subverted by its Achilles' heel, that which it most covets — Catholicism is lured by spiritual authority, Orthodoxy by sacred tradition, and Protestantism by biblical scholarship.

Only a small minority led by Pope Peter II, the Elder John, and Professor Pauli resist. They are slaughtered. With their death unity has finally been achieved. The occasion is celebrated by tongues of fire, exotic music, and the murmur of angelic, childlike, and demonic voices. The Antichrist has triumphed. But his triumph is short-lived. Peter, John, and Paul return to life, proclaim the true union of the churches, and follow the sign of 'a woman clothed in the sun' to Sinai.[24] Here the narrative ends to be supplemented by Mr. Z: The Emperor, Apollonius, and their troops are swallowed by a lake of fire. Christ descends to earth. The executed Christians and Jews rise to life and reign with Christ for a thousand years. This is the end of history, "the coming, the glorification, and the destruction of Antichrist."[25] All this takes place in the twenty-first century.

Soloviev appears to have discarded his enthusiasm for the 'theogonic process' at work in human history and the cosmos. Progress is jettisoned and becomes a herald of the End Times. The building up of the human city is transmuted from a goal to mere spadework for the advancing empire of Antichrist. The radicality of evil dispels the illusion of this-worldly

22. Soloviev, *War, Progress,* 191.
23. Soloviev, *War, Progress,* 201.
24. Soloviev, *War, Progress,* 210-23.
25. Soloviev, *War, Progress,* 227.

salvation and motivates a leap from secular progress to the eschatological. The "Short Story" becomes a chilling parable, applicable to all eras of history including our own.

*   *   *

Nikolai Berdyaev (1874-1948) stated that Soloviev was the outstanding Russian philosopher of the nineteenth century. Von Balthasar considered him the greatest artist of conceptual organization since St. Thomas Aquinas.[26] Whether or not these appraisals correspond to reality is not to be debated. However, they do point to the relevance of this enigmatic, often self-contradictory man who was said to have occult powers, a man, in Berdyaev's words, "of air, not of earth."[27] The insights provided by Soloviev were often developed by Berdyaev in a less inspired but more discursive form.

His own career was checkered.[28] Berdyaev studied at the universities of Kiev and Heidelberg and was an early advocate of Marxism, for which Tsarist Russia exiled him to the Far North. After rejecting Marxism he joined a circle of symbolists grouped around Dimitri Merezhkovski, the novelist who propounded a new religious consciousness, the 'Third Testament of the Holy Spirit' of an antinomian tilt, that aspired to restore the flesh to its rightful place in human life. Breaking with the group in 1908, he moved towards a more conventional Christianity and initiated a prolific writing career. After the 1917 revolution he taught political economy at Moscow University. He was expelled as an upholder of religion in 1922 and settled in Paris, where he directed a learned academy while continuing to publish and lecture.

While Soloviev for most of his life defended modernity and modernizing trends, Berdyaev viewed the twentieth century with trepidation, as a period of quickening decay. The decay was advanced by the effects of the Industrial Revolution, "one of the worst revolutions that has ever swept

26. Balthasar, *Herrlichkeit,* 651. Cited by Kline, "Russian Religious Thought," 217.

27. Berdyaev, *Russian Idea,* 182-83.

28. Nikolai Berdyaev, *Dream and Reality: An Essay in Autobiography,* trans. Katherine Lampert (New York: Collier, 1963).

over mankind."[29] Society, he thought, was crumbling, saved from complete disintegration only by the presence of the Christian remnant that perdures in secular form. A renaissance is possible, but it hinges on the acceptance by society of a new religious asceticism. This 'unimaginable renaissance' will be the polar opposite of an Enlightenment, i.e., any age in which self-confident reason raises itself above the mysteries of Being and Life.[30] It will be the 'New Middle Ages' to which many signs — the advocacy of a global spiritual culture, the revival of magic and occultism, the awakening of the Orient from its lethargy — are pointing.

The Christian Church must again become a force that transfigures the whole of life from within. If it does so, life will become more austere. Progress as an ideal will be discarded. Humanity will acquire a taste for eternity and turn to the supernatural . . . to God . . . or to Satan! Women, as bearers of 'the eternal feminine', will be given more importance. But Russia must undergo a 'great expiation' as "only then will its will to transfigure life give it the right to determine its mission in the world."[31]

Russians unite East and West, two worlds in conflict. They are 'people of the end' in whom the eschatological problem takes an immeasurably great place. There had long been a feeling that Russia had its unique destiny. This rose to the surface as an explicit philosophy of history.[32] Chadayev's *Apology of a Madman* (1837), for example, his quest for the Kingdom of God, was instrumental in determining the direction that later thinkers, including Soloviev and Berdyaev, would take.

Soloviev was fascinated by unity, Berdyaev by time. He believed time to be the fundamental problem of human existence as it is constantly passing from Non-Being to Being.[33] Memory, as Nietzsche had suggested, is not merely a thesaurus of the past but brings about its transfor-

---

29. Nikolai Berdyaev, *The End of Our Time,* trans. Donald Attwater (London: Sheed and Ward, 1933), 42, 57-58.

30. Nikolai Berdyaev, *The Meaning of History,* trans. George Reavey (Cleveland: Meridian, 1962), 18-19.

31. Berdyaev, *Meaning of History,* 191.

32. Berdyaev, *Meaning of History,* 52.

33. Nikolai Berdyaev, *Solitude and Society* (Westport, Conn.: Greenwood Press, 1976), 129-30.

mation by integrating it into the future and into eternity. Time is an evil caused by the Fall. It is impossible to experience the present as a complete, joyful totality or to exorcise the dread evoked by past and future.[34] However, the fact that the Christian mysteries take place in time and memory, despite the horrors it holds, suggests that man is not hermetically sealed in nature and aspires to communion with eternity.

Moreover, through memory man becomes conscious of tradition, comes into contact with 'the mystery of history', and struggles against time. The Eternal Recurrence is hardly a panacea. It is a "terrifying vision" which moves in the opposite direction and serves only to consolidate the power of time.[35] If knowledge, as Plato taught, is truly reminiscence, then history is an escape from time. While memory apprehends the nonexistent past, prophecy reveals the nonexistent future. The present era of technology is also oriented towards the future but in a perverse way which generates a strange and inhuman world. As life becomes more technical and mechanical the evil of time augments in virulence.[36]

Berdyaev does not vault to apocalyptic as does Soloviev. In his opinion there is something decidedly wrong about the Apocalypse. How can the end of time, the achievement of timelessness, take place in time, in the future?[37] Timelessness entails the abolition of the future. He concludes that this event must take place on 'another plane' which transcends the objective world. This is possible because the intensity of man's inner life can, in his view, modify the nature of time, endowing it with a new dimension.[38] The solution: Eternity!

Although Berdyaev encountered many difficulties in Christian eschatology he repeatedly affirmed that history both begins and ends with the revelation of Christ.[39] The transition from beginning to end unites the heritage of the past with the urge for self-fulfillment and requires an ever more intimate relation between humanity and divinity as mankind as-

---

34. Berdyaev, *Solitude and Society*, 135, 138-39.
35. Berdyaev, *Solitude and Society*, 140.
36. Berdyaev, *Solitude and Society*, 145-47.
37. Berdyaev, *Solitude and Society*, 153.
38. Berdyaev, *Solitude and Society*, 155.
39. Berdyaev, *Meaning of History*, 46.

cends towards divine-humanity. He strikes out against an a-cosmism that dismisses the world as ontologically unreal and rejects the Christian doctrine of the immobility of God as it is in contradiction with fundamental Christian mysteries such as the Trinity.[40]

The intertwining of man and God is illustrated both in external history and inner spiritual experience. But an element of mystery is found at the core of this relationship. Boehme is cited to the effect that in the nature of God there lies a sort of "primal dark abyss."[41] This notion may point back to the Kabbalistic notion of the *En-Sof,* the hidden source of Divinity, the Zoharic "crevice of the great deep."[42] It is most likely garnered from later sources such as Schelling or Baader and leads to Berdyaev's conception of history as an account of the genesis of God in man, and that of man in God.

Man is intimately related to nature. At first, in the pre-Christian stage, the human spirit is immersed in nature and blends with it organically. Then, during the Middle Ages, the human spirit struggles against nature. Finally, man attempts to conquer nature, to make it an instrument to further his aspirations.[43] Unfortunately, liberation from nature is bought at a great price — the mechanization of nature. The machine not only conquers nature, but also conquers man while creating a new environment that will radically modify both man and nature.[44]

Berdyaev disliked humanism, based as it is on the denial of a higher principle, as intensely as he did technology. It birthed the democratic vulgarization of culture and its propagation among the masses. Humanism is dead. Its gravediggers were Marx, who demonstrated its collective disintegration, and Nietzsche, who inaugurated a new 'spiritual era' on its sepulcher. But the hope of a new dawn is present, one that entails the final conquest of the corruptible nature of time.

The epilogue of *The Meaning of History* discusses the views of Oswald

40. Berdyaev, *Meaning of History,* 52.

41. Berdyaev, *Meaning of History,* 57-58.

42. *The Wisdom of the Zohar,* ed. Fischel Lachower and Isaiah Tishby, trans. David Goldstein (London: Littman Library Oxford Univ. Press, 1991), 1:233; 2:449.

43. Berdyaev, *Meaning of History,* 158.

44. Berdyaev, *Meaning of History,* 106.

Spengler concerning his negative evaluation of civilization vis-à-vis culture. Berdyaev views civilization as proper to the bourgeoisie: slaves of matter and enemies of eternity. To Spengler's schema of barbarism, culture, and civilization, he makes an important addition: religious transformation.[45] Hope is added to what otherwise is a wearisome treadmill.

Soloviev and Berdyaev, their Orthodoxy influenced by heterodox and esoteric currents of thought, were able to leave speculations on the philosophy of history ranging from the commonplace to the novel and perceptive. To be sure, they are disorderly, lacking any semblance of a system. Neither elaborated a full-blown philosophy of history. They did, however, provide valuable suggestions and possible points of departure for such an enterprise. To the secular thinkers of 'the end of history' these exotic Russians may seem to be great saurians lumbering about in a prehistoric landscape. To the religious-minded they are embers that have yet to be completely extinguished.

45. Berdyaev, *Meaning of History,* 137-41.

POSTSCRIPT

The End of History

> As the archeology of our thought easily shows, man is an
> invention of recent date. And one perhaps nearing its end.
>
> M. Foucault, *The Order of Things*

Perhaps, to borrow from T. S. Eliot, history will end not with a bang but with a whimper. The highly charged scenario drawn by a St. Augustine, a Joachim, or a Marx, the scent of paradise regained emanating from a Comte or a Hegel, even the twilight red and gold of a Spengler, recede into the background. The gray on gray of posthistory occupies the limelight. Seldom has a philosophy gestated in the rarified atmosphere of European intellectuality had such resonance in the outside world. One would have to return to existentialism to find a comparison that approaches the adequate.

Posthistory has attained cult status in what Allan Bloom has called "that important subdivision of the animal kingdom of the spirit — the progressivist intellectuals."[1] And it has received no little public recognition. There is a posthistorical novel, Jünger's *Eumeswil,* which has been

1. Alexandre Kojève, *Introduction to the Reading of Hegel,* ed. Allan Bloom, trans. James H. Nichols, Jr. (New York: Basic Books, 1969), x.

175

linked to the rowdy spectacle of professional wrestling.[2] To a point its impact is puzzling, as posthistory is glaringly lacking in emotion, color, or religious and eschatological dimensions. After perusing even a selection of the profuse literature on the topic, one is left with the impression that posthistory is a ponderous banality elevated to the highest degree of complexity.

However, its principal thesis is both clear and simple. History has ended. Life will continue but in a more or less animal form, without seriousness or meaning. This proposition has spawned several variations on the theme. Looking into its genealogy, it may be advisable to begin with Antoine Cournot (1801-1877), who has been called the "apocryphal Church Father of posthistory." He maintained that humanity was entering a new phase in which individual caprice will be replaced by calculation and in which "beehive discipline" will take the place of personal initiative.

Kant can also be credited with adumbrating posthistory when he indicated that history would be overcome, that bourgeoisie society would ultimately generate a different society that would preserve itself automatically.[3] Nonetheless, in spite of these anticipations, the bulk of posthistorians belong to one of the branches of Hegel's philosophy of history, often supplemented by incursions into Nietzsche. On the fringe there are others, such as Jacob Taubes and his circle, who trace their roots to other sources such as Jewish apocalyptic.

A case has been made that the first quotable use of the term 'posthistory' was given by Arnold Gehlen:

> The history of ideas has been suspended and we have now arrived at posthistory. . . . In the very epoch when it is possible to see and report on the earth as a whole . . . the earth in this respect devoid of surprises.[4]

---

2. Paul A. Cantor, "Pro Wrestling and the End of History," *The Weekly Standard,* October 4, 1999.

3. A. Cournot, *An Essay on the Foundations of Our Knowledge.* I. Kant, "Idea for a Universal History with a Cosmopolitan Intent" (1784).

4. Cited by Lutz Niethammer, *Posthistorie,* trans. Patrick Camiller (London: Verso, 1992), 2.

Posthistory was given additional impetus when Peter Brückner died, leaving a file marked 'Posthistorie' among his papers, to be used in a course of lectures:

> All the equalizing elements of the industrial milieu thus bring in their wake the shadow of 'posthistoire', a humanity whose members are alike in their 'attitudes and behaviour', their 'interests and value judgements' — the outcome . . . is a new form of reality. . . . Specificity vanishes . . . their one-dimensional reality.[5]

To Gehlen and Brückner, Walter Benjamin should be added. In the spring of 1940 he set down eighteen reflections on the concept of history. He sent them to Gretel Adorno "as a bunch of whispering grass gathered on pensive walks."[6] The first presents an image taken from a tale by Edgar Allan Poe regarding a chess automaton manipulated by a concealed dwarf. Benjamin employs it to counsel historical materialism to enlist the services of theology in its match to decide the course of history.[7] Posthistory waits in the wings.

The spark that ignited the posthistorical fire was provided by Alexandre Kojève (1902-1968) in a series of lectures given at the *École Practique des Hautes Études* in Paris between 1933 and 1939 on Hegel's *Phenomenology of Mind*. Kojève transformed the austere text into a drama that overwhelmed the audience, a drama in tandem with the darkening clouds on the political horizon. His thesis: Hegel was right. History ended at Jena. It stopped at Napoleon. The principles of liberty and equality that emerged from the French Revolution gave birth to the modern universal and homogeneous state, the end point of ideological evolution beyond which it is impossible to progress.[8]

But the end of history is neither a cosmic nor a biological catastrophe. Man remains alive as an animal in harmony with nature. Although man, 'properly so called', the free historical individual, disappears, everything,

5. Cited by Niethammer, *Posthistorie,* 7-8.
6. Letter to Gretel Adorno, April 1940.
7. Niethammer, *Posthistorie,* 104-5.
8. Kojève, *Introduction,* 43ff.

pace Kojève, that makes man happy, remains. And this state is analogous, if not identical, to the "American Way of Life," the best suited to posthistory. Civilization crystallizes — the conditions of life petrify into a self-reproducing structure that brings about the termination of freedom and meaning. Crystallization leads to the "reanimalization" of man.[9]

As Aime Patri indicates, Kojève was the first to have attempted to constitute the intellectual and moral *ménage à trois* of Hegel, Marx, and Heidegger, which since that time has been such a great success.[10] As with Hegel, history is fundamentally the history of the relation between Master and Slave; it will end in the dialectical overcoming of both — the completely free man, the End-Man. This perfected and completed man is precisely the Slave who has overcome his servitude.[11] The working slave transforms the given world by his work. While the Master provides the motive force of historical progress — terror and dread — it is actually realized and perfected by the Slave's work.[12] In transforming the world, he transforms himself.

It should be kept in mind that for Kojève (and probably for Hegel) man, not God, is the object of religious thought. God is no more than an imaginary projection of human content into the beyond. Because of this there is a definite break between philosophy, which deals with man, and theology, which reveals the universal aspect of human existence.[13] Straining towards the ideal of Absolute Wisdom they both oppose and complete each other. Absolute Wisdom reveals the 'Perfect Man' who is everything that the Christian says about God with the exception of transcendence.[14]

This ideal is adumbrated by the theological notion of the individuality of the Man-God, Christ, which realizes itself in and through the French Revolution. The evolution of the Christian world is completed in the per-

9. Niethammer, *Posthistorie,* 143.
10. "Dialectique du Maitre et de l'Esclave," *Le Contrat Social* 5:4 (July-August, 1961): 234.
11. Kojève, *Introduction,* 9, 20.
12. Kojève, *Introduction,* 20-23.
13. Kojève, *Introduction,* 71.
14. Kojève, *Introduction,* 73.

son of the god-Man, Napoleon, the creator-head of the perfect state.[15] However, Kojève's notion that the "American Way of Life" was specific to the posthistorical period and foreshadowed the eternal present future of all humanity seems to have been abandoned following a trip to Japan and exposure to a different culture.

Descombes speaks of Hegel's triumphal return in posthistory, suggesting that it was furthered by a renewal of interest in Marxism.[16] Posthistory is basically the narrative version of what in Hegelian thought is known as Absolute Knowledge, the point at which nature is mastered and society is structured.[17] Kojève maintains that the end of human time is the definite annihilation of man, the cessation of action in its full sense. This involves, on the practical level, the disappearance of wars, revolutions, even of philosophy: "but everything else can be preserved indefinitely . . . everything that makes man happy."[18] Something of a junkheap paradise.

A good argument can be made that the consequence of the 'death of God' proclaimed by Nietzsche and euphorically parroted by his followers is nothing else than the 'death of man' — the end of history. For Hegel, interpreted by Kojève, posthistory is a triumph of knowledge, a perch from which the march of time can be interpreted. But for Nietzsche it is the age of the 'last men' who luxuriate in aimlessness without end. A horror beyond desiring. Following a more optimistic vein, Francis Fukuyama's *The End of History and the Last Man* views posthistory favorably as a sort of negative utopia.

Fukuyama marks a favorable wind which is sweeping through the world. Communism has collapsed. New democracies have emerged. Totalitarianism has failed. Authoritarianisms of all stripes are on the wane. Economic miracles bolster the worldwide economy. Fukuyama actually provides a chart of "Liberal Democracies Worldwide," showing that they have increased from three in 1790 to sixty-one in 1990. This prods him to

15. Kojève, *Introduction*, 73.

16. Vincent Descombes, *Modern French Philosophy*, trans. L. Scott-Fox and J. M. Harding (Cambridge: Cambridge Univ. Press, 1980), 9-10.

17. Descombes, *Modern French Philosophy*, 27-28.

18. Cited in Descombes, *Modern French Philosophy*, 27.

speak of "the current, worldwide, liberal revolution."[19] And to propose that "the history produced as a consequence of the unfolding of modern natural science moves in a single coherent direction."[20]

Added to this, there are presently no barbarians at the gate (one is tempted to ask: and inside of the gates?). Capitalism has proven to be the only viable economic system. Liberal democracy has proven to be the only viable political system. Fukuyama endorses Talcot Parson's view that democracy is the 'evolutionary universal' of all societies, i.e., that there exists a universal evolution in the direction of liberal democracy.[21] If the present form of political and social organization is completely satisfying — and he believes it is — it can be affirmed that history has come to an end.[22] As a bulwark against the reversal of this juggernaut trend stands the "imposing mechanism" of modern natural science, "driven by unlimited desire and guided by reason."[23]

The End-Time homogeneous state rests on two pillars: economics and recognition. This is a Hegelian term that Fukuyama sees as issuing out of a struggle between megalothymia (the desire to be recognized as superior) and isothymia (the desire to be recognized as the equal of others). He believes that the former loses respectability and force in tandem with the final neutralization of nationalism.[24] Liberal democracy forged both economics and recognition, the latter by limiting megalothymia by means of a complex series of constitutional arrangements: popular sovereignty, the rule of law, separation of powers, and so forth.[25]

One is tempted to endorse Niethammer's opinion of Fukuyama's book: "One has the impression of a kind of bandwagon operetta, in which the latest world model peacefully travels the globe and van-

---

19. Francis Fukayama, *The End of History and the Last Man* (New York: The Free Press, 1992), 46, 49-50.

20. Fukuyama, *End of History,* 66.

21. Fukuyama, *End of History,* 136.

22. Fukuyama, *End of History,* 336.

23. Fukuyama, *End of History,* 203, 275.

24. Fukuyama, *End of History,* 333.

25. Fukuyama, *End of History,* 66.

quishes the evil empire."[26] This impression is reinforced by his unfortunate tendency to move from the serious to the trivial, from colloquial to esoteric speech. Fukuyama vaults from attempting to decipher Plato, Hobbes, Hegel, and other worthies to mundane observations about Woody Allen and Donald Trump. Nevertheless, he does advance some interesting views.

He stipulates that it was necessary for Christianity to abolish itself by secularizing its goals so as to attain the desired 'liberation'.[27] This process is still evident today. Moreover, Fukuyama maintains that while the First World has advanced into posthistory, the Third World is 'stuck' in history. Both worlds — the historical and the posthistorical — have parallel but separate existences with relatively little interaction between them.[28] Since the 'mechanism' of modern natural science pushes ahead inexorably, the historical world is destined to expire.

The *Narrenschiff* or "Ship of Fools" is put to good use by Michel Foucault in his considerations about history . . . and posthistory. Ships that conveyed their insane cargo from port to port — a superb metaphor! He suggests that the "wisdom of fools" prefigures both the reign of Satan and the end of the world: ultimate bliss and radical punishment: insanity as a pointer to the End Times.[29] Foucault asks, "Goya's idiot who shrieks and twists his shoulders to escape from the Nothingness that imprisons him — is this the birth of the first man . . . or the last convulsion of the last dying man?"[30]

Foucault confides that his *The Order of Things* arose out of a passage of Borges that provoked an explosion of laughter, shattering the familiar landmarks of his thought. History can also be shattered. History can change its value and rediscover one of its archaic meanings. Between the age of the theatre and the age of the catalogue, for example, a new way of connecting things to the eye and to discourse — a new way of making

26. Niethammer, *Posthistorie*, 91n.12.

27. Fukuyama, *End of History*, 216.

28. Fukuyama, *End of History*, 276-77.

29. Michel Foucault, *Madness and Civilization: A History of Insanity in the Age of Reason* (New York: Vintage, 1988), 130-31.

30. Foucault, *Madness and Civilization*, 281.

history — came into being.[31] The notion of history as "a vast stream, uniform in each of its parts, drawing with it in one and the same current all men, and with them, things and animals" was shattered.[32] This occurred at the beginning of the nineteenth century when it was discovered that nature no longer endorsed either creation or the end of the world. It follows that the human being is left without history.[33]

Foucault suggests that something new is about to begin, something like "a thin line of light seen on the horizon." One culture may be coming to a close while another is approaching from a great distance:

> It was not so much the absence or the death of God that is affirmed as the end of man. . . . The 'Last Man', since he has killed God, it is he himself who must answer for his own finitude.[34]

A tragic predicament indeed! Though man as such will disappear, Foucault envisions 'new gods', 'the same gods', swelling the 'future ocean'. Nietzsche's thought does not herald the death of God but the death of his murderer: "It is the explosion of man's face in laughter and the return of masks."[35]

Since the time of Cournot several of the posthistorians have fingered technology as accelerating the process that takes us, in Baudrillard's words, "further from all reality, all history, all destiny."[36] He puts forward the notion of a 'mode of disappearance' to substitute for the dominant 'mode of production'. Influenced by Marx and Nietzsche he endorses the 'transpolitical', no less than a 'malefic curvature' that puts an end to the horizon of meaning.[37] Once again, whether or not we can decipher its full significance, we find ourselves beyond history.

The negative utopia of posthistory takes on a particularly chilling and

31. Michel Foucault, *The Order of Things* (New York: Vintage, 1994), 130-31.

32. Foucault, *Order of Things,* 366-67.

33. Foucault, *Order of Things,* 268.

34. Foucault, *Order of Things,* 385.

35. Foucault, *Order of Things,* 385.

36. Jean Baudrillard, *Revenge of the Crystal,* ed. and trans. Paul Fors and Julian Pefanis (London: Pluto Press, 1990), 163.

37. Baudrillard, *Revenge of the Crystal,* 15, 124n.4.

convoluted form in the European thinkers, a more subdued if pedestrian form in the Americans. Fukuyama's variation has gained in popularity not because of its rigor but because of its accessibility, the way in which he successfully vaults from the scholarly to the popular. Even much of the criticism launched against his views stems from the fact that, whatever their merit, they can be comprehended by nonintellectuals. Although historicism, the belief that the course of human history can, in one way or another, be subject to prediction, has been under the critical scalpel for centuries, Fukuyama's book has added to the field an extra dimension.

Karl Popper, working on ideas he had earlier elaborated in 1919-1920, launched a classical attack in his *The Poverty of Historicism*. Belief in historical destiny is sheer superstition. There can be no prediction of the course of human history by scientific or by any other rational method.[38] Popper traces historicism — somewhat arbitrarily it must be said — to its oldest form: the doctrines of the life cycles of cities and races. These prepare the way for the teleological view that there is a hidden purpose behind the apparently blind decrees of fate.[39] He advances a cogent argument. The course of history is strongly influenced by the growth of human knowledge. But as we cannot predict by rational or scientific methods the future growth of our scientific knowledge, it follows that we cannot predict the future course of human history.[40]

From a different philosophical standpoint and directed against posthistory, Karl Jaspers fulminates against the "impermissible Gnostic speculations" of the prophets of posthistory which mute if not completely destroy human responsibility.[41] On a less exalted level, Windschuttle, attacking Fukuyama directly, censures the philosophy of history *tout court* as an illegitimate method for understanding the course of human affairs either in its Hegelian liberal or Marxist socialist versions.[42] By thus limiting the field, he reduces the value of his critique.

38. Karl Popper, *The Poverty of Historicism* (New York: Harper Torchbooks, 1964), v.

39. Popper, *Poverty of Historicism,* 160.

40. Popper, *Poverty of Historicism,* vi-vii.

41. Karl Jaspers, *The Atom Bomb and the Future of Man* (Chicago: Univ. of Chicago Press, 1963), 289.

42. Keith Windschuttle, *The Killing of History* (New York: The Free Press, 1997), 173.

Posthistory, in spite of its literary pyrotechnics, convoluted reasoning, and sheer volume, fails to excite or inspire. However, it certainly does provoke interest and spur curiosity. Even a cursory glance at contemporary society appears to justify a move in that direction. The world may well be condemned to plod along a path that holds no surprises, burdened by beings who have ceased to be fully human. The apotheosis of community. An inverse millennium.

There is one last point which may provide some consolation. In his criticism of historicism, Popper states that "it almost looks as if historicists were trying to compensate themselves for the loss of an unchanging world by clinging to the faith that change can be foreseen because it is ruled by unchanging law."[43] History points to an absence, to a void. The process of desacralization has reached its zenith. After passing torturously through many levels the Holy has been completely emptied, reduced to a mere whisper of absence, a void that cries out to be filled.

It should be transparently obvious that the present study has been written from a Christian perspective. It is tragic that the philosophy of history strides through millenia to end with the depressing spectacle of a world without God, without spirit, and finally, without man. Creation is jettisoned, with the result that human society is transformed into an ant heap. Man is thus reduced to a one-dimensional triviality. Individuality is lost in the compact mass. Religion is in chaos. Reason thoroughly debased.

Nevertheless, in spite of the encircling darkness, it may be possible through hope — which counts as theological virtue — to touch the luminosity of God and the authentic End Time. This may not quite be the surrealistic drama found in Revelation but we can be assured that, as Boris Pasternak envisioned in his *Garden of Gethsemane:*

The path of the centuries is like a parable, you see,
And in its course it may burst in flames.
In the frightening name of its power
I will freely descend in torment to my grave.

43. Popper, *Poverty of Historicism,* 161.

I will descend and on the third day arise,
And as rafts float upon river waters,
So towards me for judgement like a caravan of barges,
The centuries will drift out of darkness.[44]

44. Translation by Gary Kern.

Select Bibliography

Adams, Brook. *The Law of Civilization & Decay* (London: Macmillan, 1898).

Adams, Henry. *The Degradation of the Democratic Dogma* (New York: Macmillan, 1918).

Arendt, Hannah. *Between Past and Future* (New York: Penguin, 1993).

Aron, Raymond. *Politics and History,* trans. M. B. Conant (New Brunswick: Transaction, 1984).

Berdyaev, Nicholas. *The Meaning of History,* trans. George Reavey (Cleveland: Meridian, 1962).

Burckhardt, Jacob. *The Civilization of the Renaissance in Italy,* trans. S. G. C. Middlemore (London: Penguin, 1990).

Cohn, Norman. *The Pursuit of the Millennium* (Fairlawn: Essential Books, 1957).

Collingwood, R. G. *The Idea of History* (New York: Oxford University Press, 1956).

Fukuyama, Francis. *The End of History and the Last Man* (New York: The Free Press, 1992).

Gardiner, Patrick L. (ed.). *Philosophy of History* (Oxford: Oxford University Press, 1974).

Guardini, Romano. *The End of the Modern World* (Wilmington, Del.: ISI Books, 1998).

Hegel, G. W. F. *Lectures on the Philosophy of History,* trans. J. Sibree (New York: Dover, 1956).

Herman, Arthur. *The Idea of Decline in Western History* (New York: The Free Press, 1997).

Jacoby, Russell. *The End of Utopias* (New York: Basic Books, 1999).

Jaspers, Karl. *The Atom Bomb and the Future of Man* (Chicago: University of Chicago Press, 1963).

Kermode, Frank. *The Sense of an Ending* (New York: Oxford University Press, 1997).

Kirk, Russell. *The Conservative Mind* (South Bend: Gateway, 1978).

Lowith, Karl. *Meaning in History* (Chicago: University of Chicago Press, 1949).

McGinn, Bernard. *Visions of the End* (New York: Columbia University Press, 1979).

Manuel, Frank E. *Shapes of Philosophical History* (Stanford: Stanford University Press, 1965).

Mumford, Lewis. *The Myth of the Machine* (New York: Harcourt Brace Jovanovich, 1967-1970), two volumes.

Niethammer, Lutz. *Posthistorie,* trans. P. Camiller (London: Verso, 1992).

Ortega y Gasset, José. *História como Hístema* (Madrid: Revista de Occidente, 1953).

Pieper, Josef. *The End of Time: A Meditation on the Philosophy of History.* Madrid: Revista de Occidente, 1953).

Popper, Karl. *The Poverty of Historicism* (New York: Harper Torchbooks, 1964).

Reeves, Marjorie. *The Influence of Prophecy in the Late Middle Ages* (Oxford: Clarendon, 1969)

Schlegel, Friedrich von. *Philosophy of History,* trans. J. B. Robertson (St. Clair Shores, Mich.: Scholarly, 1971).

Schmithals, Walter. *The Apocalyptic Movement,* trans. J. E. Steely (Nashville: Abingdon, 1975).

Soloviev, Vladimir. *War, Progress, and the End of History*, trans. A. Bakshy (London: University of London Press, 1915).

Voegelin, Eric. *The New Science of Politics* (Chicago: University of Chicago Press, 1952).

Windschuttle, Keith. *The Killing of History* (New York: The Free Press, 1997).

Yovel, Yirmiahu (ed.). *Philosophy of History and Action* (Dordrecht, Holland; Boston: D. Reidel Publishing Co. 1978).

Zubiri, Xavier. *Naturaleza, Historia, Dios* (Madrid: Editora Nacional, 1967).

Index

Index

Index

193